Ron + Jo Ann

Peterson

My Soul Got Bent

*The Practical Leading
of God's Spirit
That Changed the
Path of My Life*

BY

HANS PETERSON
Doctor of Veterinary Medicine

FOREWORD BY
Pastor Charles Johnson

My Soul Got Bent
The Practical Leading of God's Spirit That Changed the Path of My Life

Visit Core Publishing & Consulting Inc.'s Web site at
www.core-publishing.com or call 1-214-926-4742

LIBRARY OF CONGRESS CATALOGING-IN-PUBLICATION DATA

Peterson, Hans D. D.
    My Soul Got Bent, the practical leading of God's Spirit
that changed the path of my life

ISBN 1-933079-01-0
    1. Leading by the Spirit;   2. Autobiography;   3. Veterinarian;
    4. Christian Living; 5. Lessons of Life.

Library of Congress Control Number: 2004113775

Printed in the United States of America

10 9 8 7 6 5 4 3 2 1

CONTENTS

∽⊗∽

LIST OF ILLUSTRATIONS

FOREWORD

The songwriter of Israel wrote, "*The steps of a good man are ordered by the Lord: and he delighteth in his ways.*" (*Psalm* 37:23)

In this action-packed story of his life, Dr. Hans Peterson relates how he became a 'good man'. Coming into this world during a howling snowstorm without the aid of the modern hospital, doctors or trained midwives, he has lived a full and rich life. Breaking from a very strong religious tradition and facing the consequences of his decision, he stood firm in his convictions.

This missionary and veterinary doctor explains the steps that brought him all the way from a state bordering Canada to a small town bordering Mexico. Leaving a successful practice to begin again displays his belief in a God who does all things well. He very candidly expresses the thoughts he had when he and his faithful wife JoAnne traveled with their children to a land of another culture and at times another language.

Whether in the operating room of his animal hospital or ministering in a jail to men sick with sin, he radiates the confidence

that pain can be replaced with health in body and soul. He shares
some very vivid stories taken from real life experiences in those
environments. From the many lessons learned in life, he passes on
seventeen of them to his family, friends and readers of this text.

Having known him from the time of his first trip into Mexico,
I highly recommend the reading of this book to young and old
alike. My life has been touched by his and for this I am forever
grateful.

PASTOR CHARLES JOHNSON
Fred Jordan Missions

ACKNOWLEDGMENTS

The author would like to thank all who contributed their support during the development of this book. A special thanks to my children and their spouses who contributed time and advice:

- ～ David Peterson.
- ～ Darwin Peterson.
- ～ Kevin Peterson.
- ～ Julie Blaylock.
- ～ Jane Leach.
- ～ Karen Briles.
- ～ Sandra Dargel.
- ～ Stanley Peterson.

> **IN HIM (CHRIST) WAS LIFE;**
> **AND THE LIFE WAS THE LIGHT OF MEN**
>
> JOHN 1:4

DEDICATION

This, my first book (and probably my only book), is dedicated to my father, my mother, and my wife. These individuals have had a lasting and beneficial impact on the trajectory and meaningfulness of this gift of seventy-one years of life, given to me by my God.

To my father and mother, Johnnie and Lavilla Peterson, who guided my early Christian life and made sure I took time for the study of God's Word and that I attended church (Barsness Lutheran Church in Glenwood, Minnesota).

My wife, JoAnne Ruby (Jackson) Peterson, attended this same church, where we met and where we were later married on August 29, 1953. Her influence and help (for fifty years and counting) have been wonderful.

SPECIAL NOTE TO ALL MY
FUTURE FAMILY MEMBERS

I pray that you find God at a very early age and enjoy a life-long personal relationship with my

God. I want to meet each and every one of you in heaven, according to the will and timing of our dear Lord, Jesus Christ. In *Psalm* 102:18 we find the verse:

> *"This shall be written for the generation to come: and the people which shall be created shall praise the Lord."*

The whole of *Psalm* 102 reminds us that God will abide forever, that He will not change, and that one day all nations will fear the Lord.

~

PREFACE

Life is a unique experience. We can live it as a self-centered pursuit of "all about me" on one extreme, or give of ourselves to causes that transcend our mere physical existence for the short time we have here on earth. This story is about the life of a man named **Hans Dennis David Peterson**, born on February 7, 1933 in Chippewa Falls Township, Pope County, Minnesota to Johan (Johnnie) H., and Lavilla C. (Dalager) Peterson.

This life, as with most people's lives, consists of activities across a spectrum of extremes described on two ends of a pendulum, from *me* to *beyond me*. By the standards of the world, this life, a span from childhood to the age of seventy-one, would be considered that of a good man. By God's standard, on the other hand, this life reached a turning point in 1965, when, at the age of thirty-two, Hans became a new creature in Christ. Prior to the free gift of God's salvation, the man, Hans, was a lost soul as described in *Romans* 3:23: *"For all have sinned, and come short of the glory of God."*

As the author reflects back, the second half of his life has been deliberately marked by the grace of God. This is the portion of his life which was invested in the cause of Christ: the part of his journey that truly makes this story worth sharing. The author's goal is to encourage others to choose the blessings of God's eternal plan for their life rather than the fleeting pleasures of this world.

Within the pages of Hans' story, you will find the answer to the question: *"What makes your heart really tick?"* You will be shown how truly low mankind is without the purifying cleansing of God, seen from the perspective of what a veterinarian observed by a fence post. *Along with the underlying theme of human shortcomings, the author trusts that his life, as described in this autobiography, will be a sub-plot to the **master plan** of God.* The details of Hans' life are articulated merely to highlight the blessings of God's redemption story for those that reach for His hand. This account will demonstrate how God's hand played a role in Hans' life even prior to the turning point he experienced in his early 30's.

The phrase *"by the grace of God"* is important because it was not any great deed performed by Hans that caused his life to be transformed, but the simple act of accepting Jesus Christ as his personal Savior as described in *John 3:16: "For God so loved the world, that he gave his only begotten Son, that whosoever believeth in him shall not perish, but have everlasting life."*

I John 1:7–9 further clarifies how God transforms lives:

> *"But if we walk in the light, as he is in the light, we have fellowship one with another, and the blood of Jesus Christ His Son cleanseth us from all sin. If we say that we have no sin, we deceive ourselves, and the truth is not in us. If we confess our sins, he is faithful*

and just to forgive us our sins, and to cleanse us from
all unrighteousness."

The title of this book, *My Soul Got Bent*, refers to how the
writer's soul, (his *inner man*, the "real me" inside) was bent
toward God by the work of His Word and Spirit. *Zechariah* 9:13
begins with the phrase: *"When I have bent Judah for me..."*

This passage foretells the coming King. The King would be
just and provide salvation for all mankind. He would be lowly by
man's standards. At one point, he rode upon a colt, the foal of an
ass. This same King can still bend, or gravitate, folks toward His
ways as they yield their hearts. What an awesome Christ!

CHAPTER ONE

Introduction

We all have stories worth sharing—stories that include love, happiness, pain, and sorrow. Too often the things we appreciate about one another are taken for granted and are never discussed and then fade from our memory. Too late, we realize there was so much more we wanted to know or wanted to tell and pass along to our loved ones.

This story is about a boy born in Minnesota, during a snowstorm, without a doctor—a boy who becomes a doctor himself (that is, a doctor for animals) and whose life is later transformed by a profound discovery and acceptance of the free and simple gift of eternal life by our Lord, the Great Healer. This is the story of Hans Dennis David Peterson, DVM. This is my story—*as of June 2004.*

As a veterinarian and a lay preacher visiting with inmates in jail all these years, I have encountered thousands of different individuals from all walks of life and in a host of unique personal circumstances. I have encountered even more animals—and the animals find themselves in just as many different circumstances as their respective owners. I have learned many lessons in life from observing both my patients and their owners.

I recall a recent event in which one of my female clients came into my office very upset and requested immediate assistance with her dog in her car. The woman was very distraught and said, *"Dr. Peterson, help me—my dog swallowed a balloon and is going crazy!"* We went out to the car and looked at a blue healer female dog in the back seat. The dog was unable to stand and was shaking all over. More, she was a nursing mama dog and was panting, drooling, and draining blood from the mouth.

"When did she have the puppies?" I asked.

"About six weeks ago," was the answer. *"There are seven big puppies. She ate the balloon this morning!"*

After examining the dog, I explained to the client, *"This condition in your dog is known as eclampsia and is a deficiency of calcium in the blood. The balloon has nothing to do with what we are seeing here."* A mere 10 CCs of calcium given intravenously immediately helped the dog. I then put her in the bathtub to cool her down. Her temperature was 108° F. at this time, so a cold water bath with ice was the next step to stop the crazy panting. Half an hour later, the dog was completely back to normal. The dog and the balloon went home, with a more relaxed client.

At certain times we, like this client with the dog, think we know what is wrong or what should be done, yet when the *truth* becomes apparent, we see that we were really off-track. At other times, we are close, but still miss the mark—life is like that. As you will see in my own life story, I was confronted with a *spiritual truth* in my early 30's that shocked my belief system. Accepting and internalizing this new truth into my heart created a turning point in my life which completely altered my journey.

This is the first of seventeen lessons learned that I wish to share with you. The life lesson learned is: *"Do not just accept your core beliefs as the foundation for your life. Research and validate these based on the Word of God—build your life on spiritual truth."*

CHAPTER TWO

Heritage

The Peterson family heritage is Norwegian. This chapter (containing the Peterson family background) complements a book written in 1982, by my uncle, Pastor Erling Peterson, *Hang on the Potatoes.*

My grandparents on both sides had a tough life. They were fishermen and farmers—hard workers all. As their descendents, those of us of the current generation did not get to know them very well. They were Lutheran, did not work on Sunday, believed in church, and believed in making sure that everyone spent the first day of the week in worship. My folks later instilled this important aspect of worship and instruction into me and into my brothers and sister.

My paternal grandparents were Matthias Otelius Krog and Alexandria (Anderson) Peterson. Matthias was born in Ostvargoy Lofoten, Norway on February 24, 1873. He stood six-feet tall. From the age of fourteen, he helped his father fish for cod off the coast of Norway. He was a good singer and had a beautiful voice.

Alexandria was born in 1872. The family actually referred to Alexandria as *Sandra*. Matthias and Alexandria were married in September 1897. They immigrated to Ellis Island and then moved to Beaver Creek in Jasper, Minnesota in September 1902. They had seven children (seen in the accompanying picture):

~ Katinka (Tinka).
~ Johan (Johnnie) Halvdan, born on May 9, 1901 (my father).
~ Mina.
~ Erling.
~ Robert (not in the picture below; he died at age 8).
~ Alpha.
~ Constance Eldora.

I do not know the actual year of Matthias' death, but Alexandria passed on in 1960.

The Matthias Peterson Family in 1911: Alexandra, Katinka, Johnnie, Matthias, Mina, and Erling.

Photo courtesy of Peterson Portrait Design.

On my mom's side of the family, Hans Solfestsen Dalager (my grandfather) was born on November 5, 1842. Hans had ten children with his first wife, Ingeborg Larson, who passed away on January 5, 1887. He then married my grandmother, Amelia Bentrud, and they lived in Pope County, Glenwood, Minnesota. Amelia Bentrud arrived in 1887. She was to be a housekeeper for the Dalager Family. Most of Hans' children were older than Amelia. When Ameila married Hans and became pregnant, there were many children from his first family still living at home. As such, I am sure, the children from my grandfather's first marriage were not really happy with my grandma. Hans and Amelia also had ten children (*that makes a total of twenty children for Hans!*):

~ Theoline (Tillie), born on August 26, 1888.

~ William (Willie) Edlows, born on May 24, 1890.

~ Cora, born on June 3, 1892.

~ Selmer Martinus, born on July 7, 1894.

~ Alice, born on June 20, 1896.

~ Herman, born on June 19, 1898.

~ Alma Lenora, born on August 19, 1900.

~ Lavilla Caroline, born on May 18, 1903 (my mother).

~ Lucille Florence, born on June 17, 1905.

~ Helen Leonora, born on December 21, 1909.

Hans Dalager was a farmer in Pope County at the time when citizens could homestead. He told men who worked for him that they did not have to plow in the dark, but he expected the plows to be moving at daybreak. He also told the workers they could put the horses up after sundown. Hans Dalager was very prosperous and was considered rich. He passed away on March 23, 1910. Lavilla was only seven years old. At the time of his death, he willed

eighty acres of land to each of his children—there were eighteen
alive at that time. My grandfather also owned a farm in Canada
with about 200 acres. My dad and Uncle Herman later traveled to
Canada to check on it, and sold it to someone on a neighboring
farm on behalf of the Dalager estate.

The Hans Dalager Family: Hans and Amelia.
Photo courtesy of Peterson Portrait Design.

My dad, Johan (or Johnnie, as the family referred to him)
Halvdan Peterson, was better know as J. H. or "The Colonel" by
those in the community. He was born in the Lofoten Islands of
northern Norway. When he was just over a year old, his parents
immigrated to the United States. They arrived by ship in New York
Harbor, went through the immigration process on Ellis Island, and
then boarded a train for Beaver Creek, Minnesota, where they
arrived on September 5, 1902. They settled in Rock County, east of
Jasper, where my dad grew to manhood. He was educated to the

6th grade. He was confirmed by the Rev. L. P. Lund in the Rosedale Lutheran Church of Jasper in 1915 at about age sixteen or seventeen, after completion of his confirmation classes. His parents lived on and rented several different farms. They worked for owners of those farms in the Jasper area.

In 1920, the Peterson Family returned to Norway (that is, except for Johnnie). Johnnie remained in Minnesota and migrated north to Sedan where he worked at the farm elevator for Emil Schluter. Part of the job was to erect windmills on farm places. During this period, dad also worked in a general store and did some horse-trading. Mr. Schluter would purchase colts and unbroken horses and dad helped to break and groom them for sale. During this period of time, many horses were needed for the farm work.

The family trip back to Norway turned out to be bittersweet for those who had returned. Matthias took another wife in Norway. My dad ended up borrowing money from a friend named Mr. Arneson of Starbuck, Minnesota to help his mother and his siblings return to Minnesota after the marriage breakup. This was a true hardship for my dad. During the course of our young lives, he periodically mentioned payments that needed to be made on this obligation note.

My dad was pretty silent about his early years. What we did learn of his childhood came from his brother's book, *Hang on the Potatoes*. I do remember Dad sharing one of his teenage stories of a time when he lived in Jasper, Minnesota. He and his friend were walking into town to take in a movie. A neighbor saw them that evening and asked them to come and help him with a job. My dad and his friend said, *"Okay, sure, we will help you!"* So, the neighbor had about 100 (140-lb.) pigs to castrate! About 8 P.M., they finally finished. They smelled so bad, that they could not go any place. After a good laugh, this neighbor took them to town and bought each of them a new pair of bib overalls and fed them supper. The neighbor, Mr. Jourgenson said, *"Someone had to catch and hold those pigs!"*

Col. Johnnie H. Peterson, 1978.

Photo courtesy of Peterson Portrait Design.

My mother, Lavilla, and most of the other Hans Dalager children went to college after high school. They went to agricultural school or *normal training* (that is a course on teaching). Some went to school in St. Cloud and some went to St. Paul, Minnesota. My mother attended agriculture school at the University of Minnesota in St. Paul and graduated in 1921. She attended summer school and taught her first class in a country school in North Dakota. She also attended St. Cloud Teachers' College and taught several years in rural school districts.

My mother was teaching when Dad met her at a school *basket social*. Such socials were annual events for rural schools and

Lavilla C. (Dalager)
Peterson, 2003.

Photo courtesy of
Peterson Portrait Design.

assisted in raising money required for bats, balls, swings, etc. The ladies brought the food baskets and the men were required to bid and buy one or they did not eat. Of course, you did not want to have someone else buy your girlfriend's basket.

My dad was the young auctioneer from Brooton, Minnesota during this time period. As a young boy, he had been enchanted with auctioneering. He spent many years practicing the auction chant. Over time, he was asked to help with the school basket social fundraisers. He would auction the baskets at these socials for free just to become better known in the community as *the auctioneer*. It worked for him, not only to become a successful auctioneer in this region of Minnesota but also to find his wife.

My parents were married on March 31, 1928, at the Barsness Lutheran Church. Their five children, including myself, are:

⁓ Robert Dean Vincent, born on December 6, 1928.

∼ Hans Dennis David, born on February 7, 1933.

∼ Ralph John Alexander, born on December 12, 1935.

∼ Lila Virginia, born on October 19, 1939.

∼ Curtis Dale, born on October 31, 1945.

In 1932, my parents began to build a farmstead in Chippewa Falls Township where they farmed. It was during the late 1940's and early 1950's that my dad began his auctioneering career in earnest. In 1953, they moved in to Glenwood, Minnesota where my dad lived until his death at age 87 in 1988.

Church was important to my dad and mom. I recall that Dad and Mom were generous, giving lots of money to church and charities. They made church an important family social outlet and it provided spiritual training for each of their children as they grew to adulthood. My dad served as the Sunday school superintendent of the Barsness Lutheran Church for 25 years. Both he and my mother were also janitors, as well as wood stove and coal specialists at this church. My father would rise early on Sunday mornings and go to church to start the furnace. He would come back home and milk the cows and do the chores and then get ready to go to church for 9 A.M. or 10 A.M. services. I recall as a boy that Pastor Thompson from our church took a real interest in Dad; they would sit and visit in the car for a long time. I don't know what they talked about...

Some of my dad's other interests included:

∼ Minnesota Centennial Committee.

∼ 4-H Club leader.

∼ Toastmaster.

∼ Pope County Historical Society.

∼ Farm Bureau.

∼ Federal Land Bank Board.

~ Young at Heart Singers.

~ Pope County Representative to the Minnesota House of Representatives (2 terms, 1960–1964).

In addition to being a schoolteacher, my mother helped on the family farm. Like Dad, she was active in church and served as a Sunday school teacher for many years. In her later years, she became very active volunteering in a retirement home in Glenwood, Minnesota—donating her sewing and quilting skills. My mother died Saturday, March 13, 2004, while living at her daughter's home in Cottage Grove, Oregon at the age of 100 years, 9 months, and 25 days. As per her wish, she was laid to rest next to my dad's grave in the Barsness Lutheran Church cemetery back in Glenwood, Minnesota.

As you can easily tell, my dad and mom were of the Lutheran faith. Regional Lutheran groups are known as districts or synods. My dad and mom were part of the Evangelical Lutheran Church (also known as the ELC). While of the same denominational faith, Lutheran groups do have some organizational differences in different regions. Despite these organizational variances, these Lutheran bodies hold a similar doctrinal basis: They accept the *Bible* as the Word of God and their creeds and confessions as a proper explanation of that Word. Their belief is built upon Martin Luther's insights from the 15th century.

Understanding the Peterson heritage requires recognizing the dominant role of a strong work ethic and the place of influence that Lutheranism had in shaping the lives of those earlier generations. The roots of the Lutheran denomination can be traced back to 1517, when Martin Luther, a Roman Catholic priest, protested against some of the doctrines of the Catholic Church. This protest, by Luther, led to his excommunication from the Roman

Catholic Church. In 1529, Luther wrote his longer and shorter cat-echisms. Other documents followed over the years to form the doctrinal basis of Evangelical Lutheranism that spread across Europe. Over time, it became the state church of Denmark, Nor-way, Sweden, Finland, Iceland, Estonia, and Latvia. It is reported that the first European Lutherans to settle in the United States arrived in 1623 from Holland. Lutheran immigrants continued to arrive over the years. From 1870 to 1910, the period of time in which my dad arrived in the United States, approximately 1.8 mil-lion Lutherans arrived from Sweden, Norway, and Denmark alone.

As Martin Luther studied the Word of God, he came to believe that *"justification is by faith alone—faith in Jesus Christ; it centers in the gospel for fallen humanity."* With this newfound belief, he concluded that the teachings of the Roman Catholic Church, in regard to what man could do toward redeeming their own souls, were in conflict with this biblical insight. This truth resulted in a turning point in Martin Luther's life.

These early insights by Martin Luther ultimately led to his rejecting five of the seven sacraments held by the Roman Catholic Church. The two sacraments that remain as part of the Lutheran doctrine are the Sacrament of Holy Baptism and the Sacrament of the Altar. From Luther's *Small Catechism,* these sacraments are defined below:

THE SACRAMENT OF HOLY BAPTISM
Baptism is not just plain water, but it is the water
included in God's command and combined with
God's Word. Christ our Lord says in the last chapter
of *Matthew: "Therefore go and make disciples of all
nations, baptizing them in the name of the Father and
of the Son and of the Holy Spirit."*

THE SACRAMENT OF THE ALTAR

It is the true body and blood of our Lord Jesus Christ under the bread and wine, instituted by Christ Himself for us Christians to eat and to drink.

The holy Evangelists (Matthew, Mark, Luke, and St. Paul) write: Our Lord Jesus Christ, on the night when He was betrayed, took bread, and when He had given thanks, He broke it and gave it to the disciples and said: *"Take, eat; this is My body, which is given for you. This do in remembrance of Me."*

In the same way He also took the cup after supper, and when He had given thanks, He gave it to them, saying, *"Drink of it, all of you; this cup is the new testament in My blood, which is shed for you for the forgiveness of sins. This do, as often as you drink it, in remembrance of Me."*

In the explanation from the small catechism, the justification for infant baptism is taken from the passage of **Matthew** that *"all nations"* are to be baptized—that is, all people, young and old. The explanation goes on to explain that babies are to be baptized because a) they are included in the phrase *"all nations"*; b) Jesus especially invites little children to come to Him; c) as sinners, babies need what baptism offers; and d) babies are also able to have faith. As part of Lutheran teaching and doctrine, infants are baptized. They believe the baptized person receives the gift of regeneration from the Holy Ghost (the Holy Spirit) as part of this sacrament.

Lutheranism teaches that in The Sacrament of the Alter (that is, communion or the Lord's Supper) they receive the blood and body of Christ. The body and blood of Christ are believed to be present *in, with, and under* the bread and wine of the Lord's Supper and are received sacramentally and supernaturally. I recall as a young boy in church the pastor says, *"This is the blood of Christ. This is the body of Christ."* Then, the pastor says, *"By the authority of God vested in me, I declare unto you the gracious forgiveness of all your sins."*

Several other key doctrinal attributes that Lutheranism centers on includes the role of: 1) the Ten Commandments; 2) the Apostles' Creed (that is, creation, redemption and sanctification); 3) the Lord's Prayer; 4) confessions; and 5) confirmation (the public confession of the faith and a lifelong pledge of fidelity to Christ).

You will see in later chapters that I did indeed build on this Peterson heritage, but also reached a turning point in my early 30's in which my core doctrinal beliefs changed, *relative to this Lutheran family tradition,* as I searched for my own answers regarding a personal relationship with my God. The *Bible* states in *John* 8:31–32:

> *"Then said Jesus to those Jews which believed on him, if*
> *ye continue in my word, then are ye my disciples*
> *indeed; and ye shall know the truth, and the truth shall*
> *make you free."*

I, like these Jews with a strong religious heritage, felt compelled to follow the instructions Jesus gave them to search the scriptures and find God's truth for themselves. The *Bible* further emphasized this point in *Philippians* 2:12:

"*Wherefore, my beloved, as ye have always obeyed, not as in my presence only, but now much more in my absence, work out your own salvation with fear and trembling.*"

Thus, the second life lesson learned that I wish to share is: "*No matter how great your parents may be (as mine were), you are personally responsible and accountable to build a biblically principled relationship with God for your own life and for eternity.*" Martin Luther did this in his day. And we see from the passages above, Jesus instructed the religious leaders of His day while He walked the earth to do the same.

～

*God has no
grandchildren—
only adopted
sons and daughters.*

～

CHAPTER THREE

Infant Years

When I was born in the Chippewa Falls Township of Pope County, Minnesota on February 7, 1933, the saying of the day after was: *"The storm brought Hans, not the stork!"*

Johnnie and Lavilla had lived on their own farm place for about a year. A small two-room cabin had been moved across the country and placed on the northwestern corner of the eighty acres Lavilla had inherited from her father.

During the summer, they added a basement room with help from carpenter friends and neighbors. The basement room had a southern exposure. There were four cement steps down to the basement level. On sunny days, it was a very cozy kitchen, laundry, and living room.

The first summer was a busy one for the pioneering pair. In fall 1931, to shelter their animals, they erected a long low shed for the horses and cattle. A straw shed was built to cover the hogs and a donkey. The donkey invariably frightened visitors with his loud, "hee-haw, hee-haw."

One February day, it looked like it would be an early spring. My parent's four-year old son, Robert, had scurried out to look for Goldie, his pet cat. In a short time Robert rushed in saying, *"Oh, Daddy! I found Goldie in the straw shed. I saw some little kittens, too."* All excited about the baby kittens and the lovely sunshine, he dashed out to see what else he could find. The false alarm of an early spring proved to be short lived.

On February 7, 1933, winter still lurked nearby, and it was in such a setting, that Johnnie and Lavilla's next baby, Hans, was to be born. The weather turned cold, dipping to zero by evening. The clouds gathered all afternoon, looking black and ominous. Fear soon dispelled the recent joy over warmer weather. Lavilla felt a twinge of pain. She wondered, would a storm come after such a mild spell? It was time for the baby any day. Aloud she mumbled, *"Oh, let the storm stay away,"* while she silently prayed for the clouds to go away.

The snow began falling. Large fluffy flakes fell steadily and by suppertime the snow had capped everything and was piling higher and higher. A slow ground wind pushed the mound gently as it played along.

Everyone had retired for the night—everyone meaning Alpha, Johnnie's sister, who was seventeen years old and had promised to stay there to keep the housework going during Lavilla's confinement, and Orville Lee, who was staying with them for a few weeks to help with the farm work while looking for a permanent job. Lorena Anderson, mom's niece, was also at the house that night.

A northwestern wind whipped and howled in our two little bedrooms. The wood-burning stove radiated very little heat. It seemed as if the fire was being sucked up the chimney. We did not yet have a plentiful supply of good seasoned wood, and the wood seemed to sizzle with moisture, not crackle as dry wood normally does.

Lavilla, who laid wide awake and alert to the sounds indoors and outside as the storm raged, worried as she became very uncomfortable with mild pains, followed by sharp pains. Lavilla moaned, *"This must not be the time for Hans to arrive!"*

The frost was becoming thicker and heavier on the windowpanes. The wind howled around the little house. The temperature continued to drop—down, down to 30 below zero—that's cold! The wind grew into a raging storm. At midnight, my father Johnnie rubbed off the frost on the windowpane. Visibility was zero. In rural areas during the 1930's there was no electricity, and the only light came from the stars and the moon. This February 7th, the sky outside was as dark as the inside of a potato sack.

A sharp pain caused Lavilla to jump out of bed. *"Oh, Johnnie,"* half sobbing and frightened, *"I believe the baby is coming!"* Johnnie alarmed, *"Oh! No! Not in this storm. The roads must be blocked; no doctor can get here tonight."*

He must try to do something. He dispatched the young man, Orville, off to our neighbor's to use their telephone to call the doctor. Our neighbor lived about a half mile away. Orville, bundled up in warm clothes, lit the lantern, which would show a small circle of light. Guided by fence posts, he followed the fence to the neighbor's barn and then made it to their house to try and summon Doctor Carnahan. Somehow, stumbling through the snow and finding his way back, Orville reported that the doctor had been called to another mother whose baby had chosen to arrive that very same night.

During Lavilla's visits to the doctor, he had informed her to be ready for an emergency. Lavilla, Johnnie and Alpha had studied the literature provided by the doctor. Lavilla had also prepared a packet with sterilized items needed for the birthing process.

The pains became sharper and more frequent. *"Why do we*

have to be without a doctor?" Lavilla felt scared for herself, her baby, and everyone else trying to cope with the difficult circumstances they reluctantly found themselves having to confront that stormy night.

One more sharp pain, could she stand one more? What must she do? Alpha and Johnnie stood by. Lavilla screamed. Johnnie calmly insisted, *"Push! Push!"* each time. Oh, a shrill cry! Oh, was it really over? Johnnie said, *"Here's your boy. What shall I do now?"* Lavilla said, *"Get the things out of the trunk. Unwrap that cloth. There is a cord, blankets, pads, and scissors."* Lavilla instructed him where to tie the cord and where to cut. The little son was breathing and alive. Alpha carefully wrapped the baby in a warm blanket and covered Mom with a quilt. Then they all waited for the doctor to arrive in the morning.

When daylight came on the morning of February 8th, it was very cold. The wind had subsided and the storm was clearing. A noise was heard downstairs. Alpha hurried to the kitchen. The doctor had finally arrived. Orville had braved the cold weather again to escort the doctor; they had hiked the long mile on foot from where the doctor's car was bogged down in a snowdrift on the highway.

My parents found out from Dr. Carnahan that the other mother that had delivered the same night as my mom was Mrs. Christianson. Mrs. Christianson, from Terrace, Minnesota, had delivered twins. These twins were Forest and Fern Christianson, who would later in life graduate from high school with me in 1951.

I received my name, Hans, from my grandfather, and I also received his work ethic. The family kept me downstairs because it was too cold upstairs. Later, when I was into everything, my temporary home was a big, makeshift wooden box. Now that's real security!

CHAPTER FOUR

Childhood Years

I remember a very happy childhood. We had no TV, so we entertained ourselves. We skied and sledded in the snow. We each had our own skis. We played kitten-ball (or softball, as it is referred to today) a lot. And, of course, we pretended we were farmers.

Some of my toys growing up were homemade, and Dad brought some home from the auction sales he called. I remember playing farm for hours. We learned to be creative because of the economic conditions of the time. We used spools (that Mom had left over from sewing) for cows and the carbon center from old flash light batteries for fence posts. Our pretend farm was under the evergreen trees close to the house. As young boys, we made our own bows and arrows from willow trees. Maybe this should not be said, but my brother Ralph would shoot them at me. *I'm sure I never returned fire!* On Saturday mornings, we listened to a radio program on WCCO, a Minneapolis Minnesota station. The program was *The Lone Ranger and Tonto.*

Life was not all play. My parents started teaching us very early
to work, and we took on increased responsibilities on the farm as
we started to mature. Dad and Mom's farming operation consisted of raising livestock and field crops, such as hay and corn, and
small grains. They always had a big garden to feed all of us. We
pumped our own water with a hand pump and Mom washed
clothes with a scrub board and homemade soap.

Contributing to my happiness as a child and throughout my
life has been my mother. She was the sweetest person on earth.
She worked hard, milked cows, carried wood, and kicked the old
motor on the washing machine (the starter was a kick pedal) until
she would cry. She and I picked corncobs for the fire. We used
wood stoves to heat the house and for cooking. These stoves had
about a five-gallon reservoir for water on one end. We kept this
full so that we would have hot water.

Saturday night was bath night. That's right—we did not have
a bath every day, as is the custom now! Mom would heat extra
water on the stove to pour into a long tin tub. We were fortunate
to have this tub because most people washed in a round washtub.
I believe Dad bought it at an auction, too, where he bought lots of
the things we used.

One day I ran to the neighbors to play with a friend, Gerald
Melby, instead of staying to help my mom pick corncobs so she
could get the stove lit. When I came home, Mom met me with a
switch. It was a memorable time because that evening my back
was still streaked and Mom felt so bad; she never did forget it.
Several times in later years, she would mention that time and how
she had cried later that night when she saw my back. "*I deserved
it, Mom!*" I probably did not cry from this experience, but hope-
fully learned that when work was to be done, I needed to be there.
A life lesson I learned here was: "*You better believe that if you*

spare the rod you spoil the child." That's the *Bible* (*Proverbs*)—
and that was true!

I was raised in Pope County, part of Chippewa Falls and Glenwood Townships, on the map below.

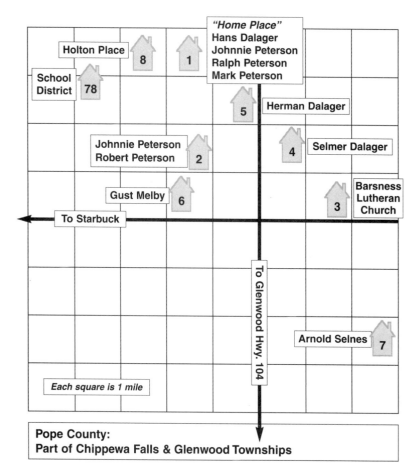

Map of Pope County, Minnesota, where
Hans Peterson was raised as a boy.

Photo courtesy of Core Publishing & Consulting, Inc.

This map shows nine key areas of interest about my boyhood days with significance to me even today. Glenwood, Minnesota, is part of westcentral Minnesota, located on beautiful Lake Minnewaska. My dad owned a cottage on this lake and we spent weekends and some evenings at this cottage. Fishing and, yes, ice fishing, were favorite past-times in this area. Walleyes and perch were the prizes.

My oldest brother Robert, next younger brother Ralph and myself were all born at the place my Dad started from scratch and is marked as No. 2 on the map. My younger sister Lila and youngest brother Curtis were born when we lived at the *Home Place*, marked as No. 1 on the map. We moved to *Home Place* when I was about six years old. My grandmother, Amelia Dalager, lived with us at the *Home Place* for many years. Amelia lived upstairs in two rooms. Grandma Amelia took care of us sometimes as we were growing up. She played cards and croquet by the hour. She spoke Norwegian and English, as did my father and mother, and often spoke Norwegian to us. I believe that she used that language when she did not want us to understand what she said. "*Stig-e-mon*" was a favorite expression of hers, and I believe it means *mean one* or *that was ugly*. Amelia had a flower garden behind a poorly constructed fence. When the chickens were in the garden, she called to them *stig-e-mon*, while waving a stick to chase them away. I recall one rumor passed down from previous generations that Amelia's mother (my great-grandma, Mrs. Bentrud) smoked a pipe. It was also widely reported that my great-grandma would bum tobacco from friends at times.

My folks and younger sister Lila and brother Curtis later lived at the cottage on Lake Minnewaska (after I had left for college) and at another location known as the Selnes farm (marked as No. 7 on the map). Lucille, my mother's sister, married Arnold Selnes and this was their home until Arnold died and Lucille moved into town in Glenwood, Minnesota. Lucille and my mother were always very close and looked out for one another over the years. I still fondly recall my 7th birthday because of a gift given by Arnold and Lucille Selnes. They came over and gave me a pocket watch, all my own. They were very special people. They were sponsors (referred to in Lutheranism as my godfather and god-mother) for me when I was *baptized as an infant.* Later in life, when my brother Ralph and Jeanette were married, they moved to the *Home Place.* Today, my nephew Mark Peterson lives on the *Home Place.*

The place marked as No. 2 on the map, that Dad and Mom originally built, was later owned by my brother, Robert, and his wife Eunice. It burned to the ground January 17, 1988. At two o'clock that morning, Robert and Eunice were awakened by one of the children, Lynn, and were able to get out with only their shoes and pants. Robert and Eunice rebuilt a beautiful log cabin style home in the same location.

The Barsness Lutheran Church is marked as No. 3 on the map. A recent photograph of this church is shown here.

Barsness Lutheran Church in Pope County, Minnesota 2004.

Photo courtesy of Peterson Portrait Design.

The Barsness Lutheran Church, established in 1867, was, and is, an important part of our lives. The first pastor, from 1867 to 1868, was Pastor Thomas Johnson. Some of the other pastors from this church over the years include: Pastor Belgium, Pastor Barsness, Pastor Thompson, Pastor Pederson (no relation), and Pastor Hooke. The current Pastor is Pastor Eileen Mehl. The number of people in attendance varied, but when I was young, attendance ranged from 50 to 150 people. I recall as a boy, on the way to church, my mother would clean our ears with a ladies handkerchief and spit. We learned that you do not run in church. We also learned that if you decided to run outside the church, you did not want to get caught. I recall some of the spiritual lessons we learned in church. The law was taught along with the *Bible* stories each Sunday, and this was repeated every year. The *Old Testament* men and prophets (Daniel, Gideon, Samson, Abraham, Isaac, Jacob, and Joseph) were known by all from my father and mother's teaching during Sunday school. **During this period of time, my parents taught me a key lesson of life from *II Timothy* 2:15:** *"Be honest with all men and study to show yourself approved unto God a workman that needeth not to be ashamed—rightly dividing the word of truth."* This principle would play a key role later in my life.

I attended school in a one-room county schoolhouse with a basement through the 8th grade. It was referred to as *School District 78* and is shown on the map accordingly. I started school at age six. My 1st grade teacher was Mrs. Abner Ogdahl and my 1st primer was *See Dick Run*. On Friday afternoons, we had *manual training*. This was woodworking or sewing. We would cut out a 'figure' with a coping saw, sand it and sand it and finally paint it. Later, we would bring it home to Mom. The wood for these projects came from the abundance of apple crates. While at this school, at recess time we all played kitten-ball; even the teacher would play. There were about eleven to nineteen students from first to eighth grade. I still remember some of these classmates: Doris Melby, Gloria Melby, Gerald Melby, Norman Austvold, Ethyl Austvold, Irene Austvold, Paul Barsness, Norma Barsness, Lester Holton, Robert Peterson, Ralph Peterson, Carol Carlson, Marlys Carlson, Leroy Hanson, the Peters boys, Morten Olson, Jim Olson, and Warren Olson. I also remember a girl who gave me a Valentine that said that *she was "as mad as a Russian about me."* I cannot remember her name…

One of my closest school pals I grew up with was a neighbor by the name of Gerald Melby. His parents, Gust and Thelma Melby, had a farm neighboring ours (shown as No. 6 on the map). Our family would visit them sometimes in the evenings. Gerald and I were in the same grade in the one-room county school district 78 through the 8th grade and then went on to Glenwood High School together. My family would also sometimes visit my uncle, Herman Dalager, (shown as No. 5 on the map) and Uncle Selmer Dalager (shown as No. 4 on the map).

While attending School District 78 as boys, Gerald and I skipped school for a day together in about the 5th grade. When we skipped that day, we roasted minnows on a little fire. We ate roasted whole minnows that day, a real treat. Gerald still claims the minnows we ate were raw! For our crime of skipping school, once we were caught, I was whipped by the teacher, a man named Mr. Koenen. Later that evening, I was again whipped by my dad. **This life lesson kept me in school the balance of my school years and taught me that: "*School is extremely important, and it is worth the effort to study hard.*"**

When we came home from school, we ate! We had lunch first and then had chores to do. This was the time Ralph and I played, too, sneaking a little time in here and there. Dad bought Shetland ponies (named Toby and May) for us when we lived on the *Home Place.* We used the ponies to go fetch the cows for milking. Toby was slow and stubborn and May was younger and very fast. Ralph rode May and was a good horseback rider. I rode Toby. One day Toby had to cross a small pond to go to the cow pasture. She went to the middle of the pond and laid down. I walked to shore and was wet to the waist. Toby turned the other way and went back home. I recall another event involving Ralph. One day our cows had broken out of the fence and wandered about two miles from home. Ralph took May to help drive them home, and as they were coming home across a plowed field, May stumbled and fell, with Ralph rolling around in the field. Dad was sure he had lost a son, but Ralph stood up and shook off the dust—he was okay!

Many of my years were spent grooming cows, herding cows, or walking to the pasture to bring them home. I learned to play a mouth organ while watching cattle.

In the fall of the year the crab apples were ripe and good. We could eat apples and ride to the pasture. I remember wild plums ripening in the fall. They were very tart, but we loved them and ate lots of them.

I recall on a particular 4th of July, Ralph and I were to be in a parade in Glenwood, Minnesota. We had a buggy, harness, and team fixed up with red ribbons and silver buckles. On the way to town, there was a bad storm with lightning and thunder like you wouldn't believe. At about Harold Femrite's place (a mile or so from downtown Glenwood) we pulled over under a tree for protection. We heard a bong-bong, a severe lightning and thunderbolt just scared us good. We jumped in the buggy and headed on for town. The parade went all right but our clothes were wet all day. At another 4th of July parade, I walked on stilts. With the stilts, I stood about nine-feet tall and was dressed in an Uncle Sam suit that Mom had made for me.

We all belonged to the 4-H Club. This was a once-a-month meeting and teaching session. We had demonstrations at these meetings. One showed how to tie knots in a rope, like a slipknot, a square knot, or a knot on a bite. Someone else showed us how to plant a tree or a strawberry plant. The officers of the 4-H Club were elected new each year. These experiences were an honor and very helpful to me in later years. The 4-H Club played a key role in my life.

There are a couple of other significant events in my childhood that would later influence my adult life. Hercules, a gray-haired crossbreed mutt, is the first dog I remember. He was run over by a car at roughly the age of eight months. It was a very sad day and my Aunt Helen helped me with the funeral. On another occasion, I had a Holstein calf that had been purchased from Holten Brothers (No. 8 on the map) who lived about a half of mile from the *Home Place*. The cost for the calf at this time was $108.25! I remember the cost because Dad paid the $108 and left off the 25 cents. The Holten Brothers made me go back for the 25 cents, and my dad was pretty upset about it.

Later that month, all the calves were dehorned, including this Holstein heifer belonging to me. About fifteen days later, my calf was hanging its head, not eating, and very sick. Today I know it was a dehorn infection that caused this prize heifer of mine to die. I was seven years old, and I determined that I wanted to go to veterinary school to try to see if there was a better way to dehorn calves so they could all live! In hindsight, as I write this book, this is another important lesson in life. **The life lesson learned is: "If** *at all possible, try to select a career in life that coincides with your personal areas of passion. This will increase your odds of being* *successful and having a rewarding work experience over your entire lifetime."* Aside from the events surrounding my everyday life, two different world events that transpired during my boyhood made a lasting impression.

The Depression Years were from 1929 through the mid-1930's. As I grew older, I heard many horror stories about this period. Stories of pigs ready for market, but worth nothing. Stories pertaining to eight to ten cows needing hay, but no hay was available. As such, early on in my life, the family was considered poor. I am sure Dad and Mom had to scrape to make it in those early years. I remember Dad rejoicing over a good crop of potatoes. They were sold for $1 or $2 per 100 lb. **A life lesson I learned from my parents during this time was:** *"We need to watch what and how we spend our financial resources in life."* Fortunately, my future wife, JoAnne, also learned these same lessons during this period of her life, and they have served us well as we have pursued our lives together.

On December 7, 1941, Japan bombed Pearl Harbor. This was a hard time for the nation and for many families in our small circle of the world. We had a flag up at our church that had about twenty-five blue stars, representing members of our church that were in the service. If someone lost their life in the war, their star was changed to gold. If I recall correctly, there were five gold stars on that flag when the war ended. During World War II, from 1941 to 1945, my mother taught gardening and homemaking. She went from school to school in Pope County and gave children tips on agriculture and home gardening. Sometimes I went along. These tips encouraged farm folks to plant *Victory Gardens* to help with the war effort.

America was united in this World War II effort. All Americans gave their best to secure freedom for all. Those five Gold Stars (along with many, many more men) paid the ultimate price to suppress the goals of global conquest and terrorism; they will always be prevalent in my thoughts. Thanks be to all those men— God bless their memories and sacrifice!

CHAPTER FIVE

Teen Years

High school was a new experience and was work for me. We rode the bus to and from school—it was about seven miles to Glenwood High. Algebra was a tough subject for me. I remember giving a declamation by memory under a teacher named Mrs. DeGroat. I sang in the high school choir. Yes, I also played football and ran track, but it was difficult to juggle that with my work at home. My long-time boyhood friend, Gerald Melby, was the quarterback on Glenwood's football team for the 1949 and 1950 seasons. I was his center during this period of time. Sometimes we would have long practices and be late for chores at home like milking, feeding and cleaning the livestock pens. I say this to defend my grades. That work ethic that was an integral part of my childhood has had a positive impact on my life. This upbringing by Johnnie and Lavilla meant their children learned to do things. We learned to make things from what was available. We could use a hammer or a saw, and we could find a bolt from a junk bolt bin to keep a broken door on its hinges.

My dad hated football. *"Dumb,"* he would say, *"Go into a huddle, come out and all fall in a pile. Then do the same thing again. Dumb!"* However, we boys would do anything for Coach Hanson. One Saturday, the city was supplying Bruce seedling trees to plant on the hillside entrance into the Glenwood area. The football team was supposed to help. That Saturday Dad was visibly upset. Go on Saturday? Saturday was a workday to Dad, but I went and planted hundreds of trees on the slope of the hill leading into Glenwood. Some of those trees are still there. Dad got over it okay, but always said that we would do anything for Coach Hanson.

Girls—not much going on in my early high school years. Socially, I was sort of shy. I had acne and that bothered me. Later, when I went to college at Concordia in Moorhead, Minnesota, I went for some help with this problem, although I probably just outgrew it.

Often Dad would come home late from an auction somewhere between seven and nine o'clock in the evening. My brothers and I would likely still be in the barn finishing up milking and other chores. When Dad got home, he would check on what was done and brag on us for doing a good job. Not all was perfect however. I recall one time he spanked me pretty good. I didn't deserve it either. All I had done was throw a bucket of milk on Ralph!

Maybe it is not funny, but Mom had problems with Ralph and I. Sometimes we got along well, but sometimes we did not. We were supposed to rake up some hay before Dad came home from an auction sale one day. We both wanted to drive the tractor, and so the fighting kept us from getting anything done. Here comes Mom, "Okay, we are going to take turns. Hans, you take one round, then Ralph." All the time, Mom stood by the field with a long stick. It was all Ralph's fault!

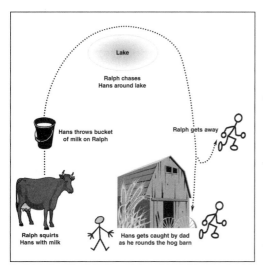

Illustration of Hans and Ralph Peterson getting into trouble as brothers on the farm. However, this was no joke—Hans got the spanking from Dad on this one and Ralph got away!

Photo courtesy of Core Publishing & Consulting, Inc.

Ronald Hanson and I played "*knife*" at noon hour in school when weather permitted. Playing "*knife*" is a lost art. Can you imagine being allowed to carry a jackknife in your pocket today in school? Hilda Bentrud, my Grandmother Amelia's sister, lived right next to the high school, so we played it on her lawn. *If you want to know how to play the game, give me a call.* My Grandmother Amelia and Tillie Ogdahl, her daughter, also lived in Glenwood while I was in high school. We sometimes would go there and wait for a ride or stay until time for a meeting we needed to attend later that evening.

Summer was spent working at home. Planting corn was Dad's job, but keeping the cornfield clean was the boys' job. Horse cultivators, both those that plowed a single row and a double row, were used a lot. My usual team of horses was Nellie and Topsy. Sometimes Nellie and Barney, but Barney was so slow. We also had to put up hay. In the fall, we helped with the *threshing run*.

My uncle Herman Dalager was a role model for me as a

teenager. Uncle Herman was the owner of a threshing machine that served our area of Minnesota. *Advanced Rumley* was the name of this machine. Herman kept things greased and running and stood at the bundle-eating end, sort of like a guard to a gate. I admired the machine and the master that made it run. It took about eight bundle racks and teams to keep this hungry machine fed. Straw came out the blower and golden grain came out the spout. The bundle wagons brought the grain from the field to the threshing machine—some had steel wheels and some had rubber wheels. These wagons were pulled by horses in the early part of my life, and later they were pulled with tractors. My horse team again was Nellie and Topsy. Topsy was on the right side because she hated the threshing machine. I unloaded on the left side of the machine.

My first job away from home was working for the Holton Brothers who lived next door. I would go there after school. This was in the days of threshing machines, binders and grain shocks. You shocked the grain from 4 to 8 P.M. and were paid 25-cents per hour. It was an important opportunity, and I was getting rich; this taught me to work on my own.

When I was growing up, children never expected to be paid by their parents. We worked because we were expected to work, and we had a dinner plate to eat at and a bed to sleep in. Sometimes on Saturday nights when the family went to town to get groceries, we would be given 25 cents to go to a movie. The movie was usually the Gene Autry and the Wild West type. We did not take vacations. On Sundays, we did go visit local people near our home: the Selnes family, the Melby family, Selmer Dalager, Adolph and Cora Anderson.

Norman Austvold was a year older than me, and we were very close friends and visited a lot together. When we started high school, Norman drove to school and sometimes I would ride with Norman instead of the bus. We dated girls together sometimes because Norman had the car. One day Norman said, *"JoAnne Jackson is really going to be a pretty girl someday."* Oh yes, I knew who she was, but I hadn't paid any attention yet.

Activities at Barsness Lutheran Church played a big role in our social and educational life as teenagers. On Sunday evenings at Barsness Lutheran Church we had devotions and readings of the Word of God, usually followed with coffee or kool-aid and a cookie. Then, we played square games. We would push all the chairs (and I guess all the adults) to one side of the church basement and square games would commence. These games included such activities as:

~ Farmer in the Dell.

~ Vis-Vas-Boom-Boom.

~ Ti Sato Vent Ve Go.

~ Candi Yeta.

Don't ask me what the words meant, but we could swing and sing to them!

Sometimes the Luther League would meet in a home when only the young folks would attend, and the parents of that home were chaperones for the evening events. Of course, we had a short devotional and later played cards or softball. At one of these card games, at Bertin Austvold's place, I sat at a card table next to JoAnne Jackson. I put my foot on hers, and she put hers on mine. We called it *footsy,* and that night I noticed the girl that Norman Austvold had mentioned earlier!

As I matured into my teens, I did turn out to be interested in that Starbuck girl, the daughter of Art and Anna Jackson, named JoAnne. JoAnne went to school in Starbuck, but we saw each other at church and community functions. We got sort of cozy on those Christmas caroling miles. The young people would go from farm to farm to sing to the old people. We thought, at the time, that some of those people were very old who had been married more than twenty-five years! It was in-between farms that we got to know each other better.

Another function in our area was *yul-a-buking*. The spelling may be wrong, but it is written like it sounds. Norwegian fun, I guess. We would dress up and present ourselves at some place with masks on. Folks were to guess who was under the masks. After everyone was recognized, they usually gave us some candy or a treat and we were off to the next place. On one of those trips between farms, JoAnne and I learned about "The Kiss", Wow!

My first car was a Model A Ford (it was Dad's truck). The back end had been cut off and made into a truck. JoAnne and I used this in my teen years to go to *kitten-ball* games. We did not go very far from home because I never knew when the truck would need to be pushed home.

I had the mumps my last year in high school. I sat or slept in bed for about 10 days. It was terrible! Before it was over, I knew where every flower and faded bud was on the wallpaper. But, I survived!

We had around forty ewes at our place while I was in high school. One day Dad brought me a sheep-shearing clipper and a chart from the U.S. Department of Agriculture on how to shear sheep. Dad had brought a Stewart Warner flexible shaft sheep shearer home from a sale. He announced that we were going to shear the sheep. After shearing one sheep, Dad said that he had to go to town and told me to do the best I could. Following the chart closely, I sheared one and then another and had about six done by the time Dad got back home. *"That's great,"* he said, *"keep working at it."*

In 1950 my steer calf for the 4-H Club was a winner in the County Fair, and the calf and I were on our way to St. Paul, Minnesota to the State 4-H Livestock Show. The first morning an announcement came across the public address system that the sheep-shearing contest was about to start. Sheep-shearing! I told my 4-H leader that I could shear sheep and wanted to enter the contest. Three hours later it was announced that Hans Peterson from Pope County was the 1950 Minnesota State 4-H sheep-shearing champ! I received a nice buckle and a trip to Chicago to compete in the national shearing bee. The Pope County Tribune on November 30, 1950, ran the following photo of me participating in this sheep-shearing event.

Hans Peterson shearing sheep in 1950.

Photo courtesy of Peterson Portrait Design, from faded news clipping from the Pope County Tribune newspaper.

So, I took a train ride to Chicago, Illinois to compete in a national sheep-shearing contest. I did not place or do well in the competition, but I met some important people. One was Mr. Leonard Harkness, the State 4-H leader for the State of Minnesota. Later in my life, he wrote a letter of reference recommending me as a student for veterinary school. Years later, my wife JoAnne would carry mail to the offices at Coffey Hall where Mr. Leonard Harkness had an office! Small world, or God's hand at work, way back in high school in my life?

So many seemingly unrelated events turn out to be interrelated in one's life. Truly, as I reflect back over my life even in those early years, I can see how God has been in control—directing, encouraging and helping to form my life and to prepare me for my family of today. **A life lesson learned, by reflecting back on my youth is that indeed, this scripture (*Romans* 8:28) is true: we know that** *"All things work together for good to them that love God, to them who are the called according to His purpose."*

Springtime brought sheep shearing and money for me. It was work, but sometimes I sheared twenty to fifty sheep in one day. Those years made me more independent. For about four years, I sheared 1,500 head of sheep in the spring at 50 cents per head. This money was saved for college and after high school it was off to Concordia with these funds I had earned while still in high school.

After shearing sheep for several years, I worked as a carpenter for Mr. Lester Ogdahl. Lester was my cousin and learned about building and carpentry during World War II. In 1948, Pope County has a bad storm. Many barns blew down. The barns on *Home Place* where we lived, at Herman's place, and at the Holton's place all blew down. There were many others damaged as well, and windmills and trees were down all over. Lester Ogdahl had much work to reconstruct these barns. One farm (the Hovdi farm) needed a new barn, but they wanted to salvage as much of the old lumber as they could off the old barn. Lester hired me as a teenager to pull nails and clean up the lumber. After this time, Lester gave me work whenever I asked for construction work. He taught me much about carpentry, and this was a blessing down the road.

During this period of history, polio had not been eradicated through the introduction of a vaccine by Dr. Jonas E. Salk in the mid-1950s. Polio touched some friends and people in our church. Hans Dalager, my cousin, and Barbara Gandrud come to mind. Both wore braces and lived with the disability.

In high school, I remember Pastor Allen Lee, a Lutheran evangelist in a wheelchair, coming to Barsness Lutheran Church to put on some special services for the youth. One of those services was based on his book entitled *My Soul More Bent*. That made a big impact on me as a young man. *Recently, I tried to find an old copy of Pastor Lee's book, but unfortunately was unable to locate a copy in print today.*

The service by Pastor Lee that made an impact on me was about contrasting individuals, over the course of their lives, to different sized nails. Pastor Lee started off with a lightweight 2-penny nail that he could easily bend with his fingers. He explained that this represented a young child. If they find and follow God as this age, God can easily bend them toward His ways. As people get older, they become like a 3-penny, then 4-penny, and onto a 5-penny nail, etc. The evangelist illustrated that with each thicker sized nail it become increasingly more difficult to bend these nails. He used tools such as pliers to help bend the nails as they got thicker. He explained the parallels for us not allowing God to get a hold of us at a young age: it becomes more difficult the older we get. He concluded with bending a large bolt (or nearly a 20-penny nail) in a vise with a hammer pounding it over. While he strained to bend this bolt, he explained that this represented a grandpa. While it was not impossible, his point of letting God bend us toward His ways early certainly made its impression on me.

Pastor Lee made sure all teens were seated in the front rows, and he told us how important it was to read God's Word every day. Many of this teen group promised to do just that. We promised to read one chapter in the *Bible* everyday. All through high school, at bedtime, I would take time to read God's Word. The promise I made to this evangelist stayed with me. I remember getting a special light on my bed so it was easy to read. From this reading of *Bible* stories, Christ's teaching and miracles became very familiar to me. I kept that promise, and by 1959 when I completed vet school, I had read the *New Testament* 5 times. Another young lady made that promise at the same meeting: JoAnne Jackson. Later on, as I share with you how God came and looked on my family, and me this *Bible* study time will take on new meaning. From 1950 to 1951, I was leader of the Barsness Luther League.

One passage I studied during high school that reminded me of Pastor Lee's sermon on the different sized nails can be found in *Zechariah*. In fact, it is the inspiration for the title of this book, along with the ministry of Pastor Lee. *Zechariah* 9:13 states:

> "When I have bent Judah for me, filled the bow with Ephraim, and raised up thy sons, O Zion, against thy sons, O Greece, and made thee as the sword of a mighty man."

Zechariah 9 speaks of the King's coming. He would be just and provide salvation for mankind. He would be lowly by man's standards. At one point he rode upon a colt, the foal of an ass. This King can still bend folks for Himself like He did with some of us young teenagers those many years ago. This book, *My Soul Got Bent*, refers to how my soul, my inner man, the real me, was bent toward (submission to His will) God by the work of His Word and Spirit.

A key life lesson I learned at that time is: "*Young people can spot the genuine article and will bend (gravitate) toward it with the right leadership from key adult role models.*" This was demonstrated by our response to Pastor Allen Lee.

CHAPTER SIX

College Years

I graduated from high school in 1951, and my high school grades were not very impressive. I was a C student at best and was told by a recruiting officer from Concordia College during my senior year that I was not college material. Nevertheless, I would be in Moorhead, Minnesota the next fall at Concordia College.

Pre-veterinary courses were my goal at Concordia College. They had some science courses, but not the program I needed. My main courses were biology, comparative anatomy, and microbiology, sprinkled with English and religion.

In comparative anatomy we studied the *Dog Fish Shark* and I was introduced to evolution. Concordia was a church-sponsored school, and this subject confused me. *"Don't they believe that God made us like the Bible says?"* I pondered this question one day as the professor took the heart out of a frog and put it in a Petri dish. This heart was bathed in a liquid of sugar water and it continued to pump for a long time (maybe an hour). *"What makes this heart pump?"* I asked. Dr. Fugelstad explained that there is a node in the heart called the *sino atrial node.* The impulse starts there and travels through perjingi fibers to all parts of the heart and causes it to contract. *"Great,"* I said, *"But, what triggers that trigger?"* No answers were given to this question on that day. I would later find the answer, and it would play a role in a major turning point in my life.

Dr. Torstveit was the anatomy teacher and spent time teaching us about all the bones. One weekend at home, a sheep died in Dad's flock. Working all weekend Mom and I cooked the meat off of these bones until I had a skeleton. Not a skeleton, really, just a box full of bones. I brought this box to school and started assembling the bones with wire and glue. My goal was a complete skeleton of a sheep.

Traveling home from college was getting more and more exciting. JoAnne and I were getting pretty serious. She was the most beautiful person I knew, and I wanted to be with her all the time. She was to graduate from high school in 1953. Her parents, Art and Anna Jackson, were good to me. Sometimes I would help Art haul hay from the fields to the barn. Sometimes we would go with Anna ice fishing.

Now, Anna really liked to fish. In fact, Anna fished a lot with a real special friend of the family, Cora Swenson. Obviously, Cora and other individuals mentioned in this book may nave no significance to you personally, but visualize Cora in the following manner. Think back in your own life to that special aunt, uncle or family friend that was there for you in your formative and/or your adult years. Cora was such a person for JoAnne and I.

JoAnne played the lead lady in the school play in 1953. I came home from college to be there that night, and she did a perfect job. That fellow that played the main role made me a little nervous, though. He was tall and pretty good-looking. JoAnne went home with me, however, and made my day.

Back in school at Concordia, many spoke of the importance of mission outreach but few seemed to go or do this mission thing. One weekend I decided to go to Front Street in Fargo, North Dakota. Fargo, being the sister city to Moorhead, was just a walk across the river. Front Street is known as the *wino* part of Fargo— drunks and drinking defined Front Street. I brought some Lutheran gospel tracts from campus and went to visit the mission on Front Street. The man running the mission welcomed me and was glad to have help. I stood on a street corner and handed out some tracts. Another person was doing the same thing across the street. Crossing the street, I spoke to this individual and he began to teach me about his religion, the Bahai faith. When this man left, I was a little confused and wondered out loud "what is right?" Immediately, the verse from *Acts* 4:12 came to me: *"Neither is there salvation in any other, for there is none other name under heaven given among men, whereby we must be saved."*

What a blessing that the Word of God can guide and lead us into truth. I knew his beliefs were wrong and God's truth was good enough for me.

I was almost done with my skeleton of the sheep, but some small bones I needed were not in the box. Those small bones in the fetlock area had been thrown away with the soapy water we used to make the bones white. I went to the local butcher shop for help. The butcher at his shop questioned me, *"You want just the bones?"*

"Yes!" I then explained about the skeleton and he supplied me with three legs from hock on down. The bones were cooked in the dormitory with a hot plate, and by the time the smell was real bad

and filled the hallways, the bones were clean and ready to be wired. The Biology Department thought the skeleton looked pretty good and paid me $45.00 cash for the old sheep. After my dad found out what it sold for, he complained because healthy lambs were only bringing $35.00 at the market price.

In March 1953, I called JoAnne in Starbuck on an 8-party-telephone line and asked her to marry me. Tillie Jackson, JoAnne's aunt, was listening on the phone and could not hear all of our conversation. So, she called up JoAnne's mother, Anna, to find out what she had missed! JoAnne said "Yes" and started planning a wedding for August of that year. More precisely, the plans were for August 29, 1953. At a jewelry store in Moorhead, I found a diamond for $45.00 (earned from the sale of the sheep skeleton) and brought it home to JoAnne the next weekend. Some said I worked to the bones to get her. What a blessing she has been! We really have it for one another. If you recall the comment from Norman Austwold, he was right; she was beautiful! I love you Jo (my short name for JoAnne)!

College work went all right and C's and B's allowed me to stay with it. Concordia was a disappointment, however, because they really didn't supply the pre-vet courses as I had hoped. By my sophomore year, this was obvious, and I transferred to University of Minnesota, St. Paul campus. During the summer of 1953, I worked with sheep shearing and carpentry to get more money for college and to support my upcoming marriage.

Due to my experiences during the Concordia College days of 1951–1953, I felt that I grew up some as a person. I had to work in the cafeteria to help pay for college. In the cafeteria, sometimes I worked in the bakery and other times running the dishwasher or preparing mashed potatoes in pots as big as washtubs. Those ladies in the cafeteria were very kind and patient with me. They strengthened my work ethic, and some of the other cafeteria workers were good campus friends. At one difficult time at Concordia, I had a big decision to make; I called on God for His help. *"God, if you will help me with this problem, I will preach the gospel."* God did answer that prayer, but I would forget this promise until 1965. More discussion on this later.

I bought my first car. It was a 1939 Mercury that had very little compression, but I drove it to Carrington, North Dakota to shear sheep. That turned out to be a big mistake because all the flocks of sheep were big (500–800 head or more!), and the farmers wanted a shearing crew so the work would go faster. To survive and buy gas for the '39, I worked in a wool-buying store for about one week. The warehouse was full of fleeces that needed to be bagged. These bags were big, 8–10 feet tall and 5 feet in diameter. The boss man said, *"Throw the wool in the bags and tramp it down with your feet."* The warehouse was warm, and it had to have been the most difficult work I had done. When I called Dad one night, he said there was plenty of shearing at home. I was glad to get home to shear on my own and to see more of JoAnne.

The wedding day came and the ceremony was at Barsness Lutheran Church. Anna Jackson, Lucille Selnes, Emmitt Jenson (a friend of the family), JoAnne, and probably many others from the church helped to make it pretty and nice. We had flowers (lots of flowers) and mosquitoes. After our wedding, the church bought screens for the windows because so many suffered from the mosquito bites. JoAnne and I really didn't notice the mosquitoes, but JoAnne's veil still had many mosquitoes caught in the mesh when we examined it in 1968 prior to our move to Texas.

Lucille Selnes made a beautiful angel food cake and a reception followed downstairs in the church. We had many young men at the church for our wedding, Ralph Peterson and Gerald Melby, naming only two. The 1939 Mercury was out of order by the time we were ready to leave the church after the wedding ceremony. That car could hardly run on six good plugs and someone pulled one wire off. We later found out that the manifold was smeared with Limburger cheese. *"Who would do something like that? Again, did I mention that Ralph and Gerald were at the church?"*

Art Jackson saved the day for me. He handed me the keys to his car and said, *"Have a good honeymoon."* What a father-in-law! And I might add what a mother-in-law. They were most support- ive and helpful to us as we were getting started. In the following summer (it was then 1954), while I was out of school, JoAnne and

Hans and JoAnne (Jackson) Peterson married at Barsness Lutheran Church in Pope County, Minnesota on August 29, 1953.

Photo courtesy of Peterson Portrait Design.

I stayed upstairs in their home, and I am sure that was not easy for them. Our first child, David, was born in July 1954 while living in their home as well.

JoAnne and I spent three days in north Minnesota at Whispering Pines Resort. We promised each other that we would put Jesus Christ and God first in our lives. We were never sorry for that early start with God. Our wedding picture from August 29, 1953 is shown here.

After our marriage, I enrolled at the University of Minnesota, St. Paul Campus, and that is where JoAnne and I headed in September of 1953. We lived upstairs in a small apartment and JoAnne made it a home. This apartment was at the corner of Como and Raymond Avenue, St. Paul, Minnesota, and the apartment was owned by Mrs. Johnson. The next fall (1954), we moved downstairs, and to get free rent we were to feed and care for Mrs. Johnson. That was a big mistake. Mrs. Johnson told JoAnne, *"I like Hans and David (our first child), but I don't like you!"* It was a real trial in our life, but we stuck it out for nine long months. Besides school and work, JoAnne and I were now caring for our first child.

We moved many times since 1953, but wherever JoAnne was became our home. She always kept the home clean and made certain that the beds were made and the laundry was done. Over the course of our marriage, she was pregnant for 72 months!

Two weeks before school started I got a job with a contractor helping lay bricks. My job was to mix the mortar and carry the bricks to the mason. That job taught me first hand about unions. The union bosses were very independent and cared only about themselves. If the carpenters had not built a scaffold for the mason, the mason just sat. He would sit for two days. What a waste!

School started for me, and JoAnne landed a job working at

Coffey Hall, the administration building of the St. Paul Campus. She distributed the mail to the two-story building. As stated previously, Mr. Leonard Harkness (the 4-H Club leader for the State Minnesota) worked in Coffey Hall.

One class that was needed to get into veterinary school was an agriculturally based-electrical engineering course. This class was a real frustration, and my final grade was F. This class was a two-quarter class. The first quarter was to prepare you for the second one. I was really let down, and I didn't know what to do. I went to my advisor for help, and he told me I would have to take the course again next fall. While a challenge, I made an A in my retake of Engineering 101 in September 1954, followed by an A in Engineering 102 the winter quarter that followed. I was then on my way to apply for veterinary school.

JoAnne and I were able to go home each March for the summers of 1954 and 1955. Sheep shearing gets started in March, and I was able to shear sheep the spring of both these years and then work in construction for Lester Ogdahl. Those two summers at home in Glenwood turned into a blessing because it gave me tuition money and then some. I sheared between 1,600 and 2,000 head during those two years. In May 1955, JoAnne would go with her parents to Glenwood for a Saturday money drawing. The winner of the drawing had to be present to win. One Saturday, JoAnne won $200 and immediately bought a washing machine, the ringer type and two tubs. That was a real blessing because she had been washing diapers and clothes in a little diaper washer. This machine was smaller than a four-gallon bucket and had two agitators that swished in the bucket from a motor in the lid. The Jackson family's lucky streak continued when JoAnne's dad won the drawing the next week for $80.

In September 1955, I started veterinary school at The College of Veterinary Medicine, University of Minnesota, St. Paul, Minnesota. The acceptance letter came in June, and JoAnne and I were both very excited. By now, children started arriving. I remember telling my dad when I got married that we were going to wait to have children until school was finished. But, the children didn't wait! I used to tell my children that they were all planned. When JoAnne and I found out she was pregnant, we started to plan! Let me also say that each and every one was a blessing and still is today.

Veterinary school was hard and a real challenge. I studied with two classmates: Rollie Jeans and Tom Wanous. Usually they came to our small army barracks-style house. Our children had to go to bed early. JoAnne was an expert at getting them settled down about 6:00 P.M. and studies usually lasted until 11 or 12 each night. My job cleaning the large animal stalls at the vet clinic started about 6:30 A.M. Pete Franz, also a classmate, helped with this job. If there were cows to milk, Pete would get me to milk them for him if it was his turn. This favor bought a donut (glazed!) before going to class.

The last two summers of vet school (1957 and 1958) I worked in the vet school as well. I worked cleaning animal stalls in the morning and again at night and helped the clinicians during the balance of the day. This was a big plus for me because I knew the routine, had an opportunity to watch how different surgeries were handled, and saw the various disease conditions in cattle and horses presented to the Minnesota Teaching Hospital during the summer months. Some of my heroes as teachers at the clinic were: Dr. Arnold, Dr. Useneks, Dr. Mather, Dr. Lowe, Dr. Zemjanis, Dr. Wolf, Dr. Perman, Dr. Larson, Dr. Griffith, Dr. Ketchum, Dr. Pomroy, Dr. Thorpe (whom I knew even though he was not a teacher of mine), Dr. Schwartzman, and Dr. Hoyt.

Dr. Hoyt and Dr. Arnold were both good to me and had confidence in my work. Dr. Usenick and Dr. Zemjanis were also on staff at the clinic during the summer months that I worked there. They took time to explain things to me and let me do more vet work than I deserved to do. Thanks, fellows!

While I was attending college, JoAnne's mother passed away on July 11, 1957. Anna Jackson was buried in the cemetery next to Barsness Lutheran Church. Our 3rd child was only three months old at the time and our oldest child was four years old; so our children did not have the opportunity to really know Grandma Anna prior to her death. However, many of our older children still remember Grandpa Art. He always had spearmint gum in his pocket, which he handed out as soon as he stepped out of his vehicle. It was not just the gum that drew our children to Art, like a magnet, he was a man with a very kind heart. Besides JoAnne, Art and Anna Jackson had another daughter and two sons:

- ∼ Arthur (Sonny) T. Jackson, born December 20, 1926 (wife, Marilyn).
- ∼ Shirley R. (Jackson) Moe, born May 26, 1933 (husband, Lawrence).
- ∼ JoAnne R. (Jackson) Peterson, born February 11, 1935 (my wife).
- ∼ Gerald H. Jackson, born November 7, 1939 (wife, Marianne).

JoAnne worked at home taking in baby-sitting jobs for other working mothers. At one time, we had four of our own children plus one Chinese and one Black child in the little yard. I remember one man walking by one day, and he said it looked like the United Nations out in our yard.

JoAnne and I were poor when I was in school, but we didn't

view it like that. Several times we had no money for food. On those occasions, I would call the University hospital and see if they needed blood donations. My blood type was A negative and brought $15.00. If we really needed the money, they always had a need for my blood type. If we were not flat broke, they didn't seem to need the blood at that particular moment.

Another job of mine while in college was cutting hair. I started giving people haircuts at Concordia College and had several regulars in vet school as well. The going price was 50 cents, the same price I charged for shearing sheep. One classmate, Tom Wilmus, came regularly for a haircut. He also studied with me and several other classmates. When we were seniors, Tom had a party at his dad's place and invited all the classmates. JoAnne and I went, and when we arrived at the house with the proper address on it, JoAnne wouldn't let me pull into the driveway. *"This can't be right,"* she said. There was a seven-car garage and a three-story mansion at the address he had given us. We found out that Tom was a millionaire even before graduation—50-cent haircuts, Wow! The dining area in Tom's mansion had a table about twenty-two feet long. There was a button on one end to call the butler. We really had an evening. Thanks Tom and Rita, we enjoyed ourselves.

Some other jobs that we worked at during those college years included:

~ Sweeping a big warehouse at night that was a construction material testing laboratory. Some nights, they would have busted a cement culvert, a cement pillar, or blocks that need to be cleaned up.

~ Milk quality testing laboratory. Here, I counted bacteria in milk samples that were sent in from around the state of Minnesota.

～ Veterinary clinical laboratory. Here, I fed guinea pigs and rabbits and kept them clean. I worked this job during summer 1956. Also located in this laboratory was the distemper ward for dogs. This allowed me to see dogs in all stages of the dreaded disease.

～ Sweeping the fair grounds during the Minnesota State Fair. This job only lasted one week in each of the summers of 1957 and 1958. All workers were required to pay entrance fee and show up for work at 10 P.M. This was a problem for us *cash-poor* vet students. However, because the fair grounds were behind the vet school, we climbed over the back fence to avoid the fee.

We started veterinary school with $200. One of the vet tools I was able to buy my sophomore year was a 1-ocular microscope for $200. It is still in working order, and I use it to this day. In 1959, when I graduated from vet school, we still had $200. Now, as I look back, I can see how the hand of God helped us along this educational journey.

As a student, I gained self-confidence as I learned new procedures and saw how different medical drugs worked. With this self-confidence, communication with people became easier as I went along. By graduation time, I knew that veterinary medicine was what I wanted to do. My college years are summarized below:

～ Concordia College: Moorhead, Minnesota (1951 to spring 1953).

～ University of Minnesota: Pre-Veterinary Bachelor of Science (fall 1953 to spring 1955, graduated on June 15, 1957).

～ University of Minnesota: Doctor of Veterinary Medicine, University of Minnesota (Fall 1955 to Spring 1959, graduated on June 19, 1959).

The Pope County Tribune newspaper ran my picture on May 28, 1959, as shown below, announcing my graduation from veterinary school.

Graduation photograph of Hans Peterson from veterinary school, Minnesota, 1959.

Photo courtesy of Peterson Portrait Design.

On July 8, 1959, the Veterinary Medical Examining Board gave me a license to practice veterinary medicine in the state of Minnesota.

CHAPTER SEVEN

Central Minnesota Career Years

From 1959 to 1965, my dad was farming and auctioneering and my mom was still teaching school in Hoffman, Minnesota. She stayed there during the week and went home on the weekends. JoAnne's mom had passed away while I was in veterinary school, but her father was farming.

My grandmother on my dad's side, Alexandria (Sandra) Peterson, lived in Jasper, Minnesota until her death. In 1960, JoAnne and I attended her funeral. She was buried at Rosedale Cemetery next to the Rosedale Lutheran Church in Pipestone County, Minnesota. The Rev. L. P. Lund presided over the service. This is the same pastor that presided over my dad's confirmation service when he was a boy attending this same church in Jasper years before. As discussed before, my grandfather Matthias Peterson had moved back to Norway; he was not part of our lives.

My grandmother on my mom's side, Amelia Dalager, lived in Glenwood in her later years in a small house purchased for her by her son-in-law, Charles Thomas (Helen's husband). Amelia passed away in 1963 at the age of 94. Hans and Amelia Dalager are buried in the cemetery at Barsness Lutheran Church.

After graduating from vet school, JoAnne and I moved to Wheaton, Minnesota to start my veterinary career and raise our family. We moved into an old house and everyone told us we would freeze in the winter. One room was my clinic, and the rest of the house was our living quarters. However, most of the veterinary work would be done on the road, driving from one farm to the next. When we were unloading the truck (my brother's truck) a client came to see me and wanted me to work on some calves the next week. Dennis Keller would be among one of my first clients, and he lived near Tintah, Minnesota. This business was started on July 14, 1959.

My first call in Wheaton was about a deer. Seems a tame deer had taken up with some cows, and the cows were afraid. The cattle ran around the pasture and the deer followed them. This farmer wanted it stopped. The game warden was involved and wanted the deer put to sleep, so it could be hauled to a wooded area about eight miles away. Because the deer was tame, it followed the farmer into a small barn and he slammed the door shut. I was young, and I foolishly went into the barn to rope the deer. When I put pressure on the lasso rope, the deer came at me front feet first. It was a very dangerous situation, but I was able to jump out of the way, to snub the deer with the rope around a post, tighter with each jump. Finally, I threw the deer to the ground. I called for help, and four other men came and helped me hold the deer as I injected an anesthesia. We loaded the deer on a pickup truck, and the game warden was off to the wooded area. He later told me that the deer slept for fourteen hours.

The newspaper that Friday ran the headlines "*New Veterinarian, Hans Peterson helps relocate deer that was stamped-*

ing local livestock." With that kind of free advertising, my practice was off and running in short order.

That first month I remember a couple of things. One was that a drug company agreed to give me credit. An initial order of $800 could be paid in three monthly installments. That certainly does not sound like much now, but at the time it was a really large commitment for a startup business.

The first cat that we had to do surgery on will always be remembered as well. In those days, we put cats and dogs to sleep by giving an IV (intra-venous injection of anesthesia) in the leg. JoAnne was my assistant, of course, and had never held a cat for a veterinarian. When the cat went to sleep, JoAnne said, *"I need air."* She opened the door and sat down on the steps. After five minutes or so she was all right. She said, *"My legs feel like rubber."*

That was the start of a wonderful veterinary assistant career, and except for several days off to have babies, she has worked for forty-five years straight. All the cleaning, washing towels, sterilizing surgical instruments, maintaining records and book work, in addition to all the housework and helping eight children with school work was an awesome accomplishment by my wife and mother of eight! She is a miracle woman: What a wife! What a veterinary technician! What a helpmate!

Those Wheaton years, 1959 to 1963, went very fast. I drove about 30,000 miles each year, mostly on gravel roads. I made some veterinary mistakes but helped some clients and animals along the way. One day a sow (pig) was having problems pigging so I drove in the yard and gave the sow a shot of Ergonial (a drug that contracts the uterus). I told Mr. Merton I would be back after I looked in on a cow at a farm up the road. When I came back in about one hour, Mr. Merton wanted to know, *"What did you give the sow? She has had six pigs since you left, and seems to be done."*

"Ergonial, eh! " I thought. That was the first time I had used the drug, but it would not be the last.

One evening, I was called to see a Holstein cow that had a plugged teat. *"We can't get any milk from this one teat, Doc. Can you open it up?"*

"Well, yes," I responded. I had just purchased this new teat knife for this problem. I inserted the blade and the cow kicked. I jumped back and watched that teat deliver about one gallon of milk onto the floor in just 20 seconds. I had slit the teat open and now the hole was too big.

The owner said, "That's okay, Doc. We can handle it now." Later he told me that if he milked the cow first, he could catch the milk before it all ran in the gutter. *"Sorry!"*

Hog vaccination was done on most farms when I first graduated from school. We vaccinated with live virus hog cholera and an antiserum, and we also vaccinated for a disease known as erysipelas. To handle this job we had a serum bag like an old-fashioned hot water bottle bag. It was attached to a hose and had an automatic syringe. The live virus was in a second syringe and the erysipelas vaccine in a 3rd syringe. All vets, including myself, became proficient in handling these three syringes. Some mornings we would vaccinate 100 to 200 head with this syringe system.

Live virus hog cholera vaccine was later removed from the market because it became apparent the live virus used was actually causing the disease to spread from farm to farm. When hog cholera did strike a farm, it would kill about 80-percent of the unvaccinated hogs on the place and then move down the road and do the same thing on the next farm.

Pregnant unvaccinated mother sows would be moved to a place where all hogs had been vaccinated and would not have any problems. But, when they had their baby pigs, most of the babies would die from hog cholera before they reached six weeks of age.

Treating calcium deficiency or milk fever in the dairy cow was always very satisfying. After calving, these cows became paralyzed and in a comatose state. When given calcium, these cows would wake up, get up and start eating.

The Wheaton practice provided me with much experience that has served me throughout the remainder of my career. Not only did I learn much about veterinary medicine, but it provided the foundational aspects of running a successful small business with my wife. Her involvement was and continues to be a critical element of my success in my various business endeavors.

In 1963, JoAnne and I decided to sell our Wheaton practice and move to Morris, Minnesota to commence another practice of veterinary medicine. We decided to undertake this change by joining in a partnership to ease the pressure of day and night working to cover all of the emergency calls. As a sole proprietorship operation in Wheaton, I could not rotate out with a partner to get some time off periodically from the constant emergencies that accompany the profession of veterinary medicine. Even so, veterinary medicine was exciting to me. I enjoyed the results of the treatment and interacting with the diverse group of clients that I came in contact with in my practice and solving the medical problems of their animals.

Starting on August 1, 1963, Dr. Al Trumble and I were partners in a veterinary practice in Morris, Minnesota. We called our practice Morris Veterinary Clinic and worked out of a new clinic built by Al and his wife, Jan, before we had moved in Morris. It was a general practice, meaning cattle, swine, horses, and pets were all accepted by the clinic. We had an office manager named Lloyd Tonn who answered the phone and manned the 2-way radios to our trucks. Lloyd kept our clinic and reception area spotless and was always there to help with a dog or cat. Lloyd also sterilized equipment as needed for surgery. The veterinary practice at Morris was very similar to the one we had in Wheaton. Some of the farms were bigger and had larger feeder pig or feedlot operations. The diseases were the same, and we continued the so-called fire-engine type practice. The client would call with a problem, and we would drive to their place to put the medical fire out.

I was very busy with work, active in our local church and supporting JoAnne as we raised our family together. We had a new home next to a small lake in a very nice neighborhood with lots of young children for ours to play with. That is, until the salamanders came out of this lake once a year! It seemed that life's trajectory for Jo and myself was set for the future. *But God had a different plan for us . . .*

CHAPTER EIGHT

The Turning Point

One day in July 1965, a man came to the clinic whom I had never met before. His name was Andy Joranger, and he was a TV and appliance repairman in the Morris area. He was in the office speaking to Lloyd when I walked in. Andy looked at me and said, *"There is nothing to baby baptism."*

"Oh, is that so," I said, and Andy laughed very loudly. He introduced himself and shortly excused himself and left.

It was noon and I went home for lunch, and I told JoAnne about Andy and said, *"There is nothing to baby baptism!"* Jo Anne said, *"I don't want to meet that man."*

I went back to work making farm calls, but about two days later we were invited to Al (my partner) and Jan Trumble's house for coffee and ice cream. You guessed it. Al's TV wasn't working and Andy was there to fix it. After checking the TV, Andy came into the living room and sat down to visit. On a coffee table in that living room was a big *Bible*. I picked it up and handed it to Andy and asked him, *"What did you mean the other day about baby baptism?"* Andy opened the *Bible* and began to teach.

First he covered *Galatians* 2 and 3. He explained the purpose of the law. *Galatians* 3:24 states: *"Wherefore the law was our schoolmaster to bring us unto Christ, that we might be justified by faith."*

Wow! I thought the law was my rules to live by. For twenty-four years, I had studied the law and never understood its purpose. The law is merely to show us that we need Christ. We cannot live it by our own strength. Justification is by faith not by our attempts to try to live the law by our own human power. We ate ice cream and started home. JoAnne spoke first and said, *"If I were to die tonight, I would go to hell!"*

We both knew we had to do some homework and study God's Word to find the real truth. We were hungry for the truth and for the real meaning of life and had seen it in action that evening. Andy did not drop the ball or leave us in the dark about the questions he had raised that night. He started dropping by our home to study the *Bible* with us, helping us to further comprehend God's Word. Andy came in the evenings and at noon, left a verse or two for us to read, and then went back home or to work.

John 1:4 it states: **"In Him was life and the life was the light of men."**

That verse came alive! Remember way back in school when the frog's heart continued to pump, and the teacher said that a little node triggered the impulse. What triggers that trigger? The answer was in that verse: "in Him was life!" His life was the light of men! I was beginning to learn the most important lesson I would ever learn.

I knew that light is a frequency and could now see that there was a frequency of light or energy coming from God to make my heart pump. If God decided to cut the wavelength or disrupt the frequency, my physical life was over. And so, I owed my life to Christ who is that light. Just let me say, He (Christ) is in control of that node in your heart as well.

John 1:12 states: *"But as many as received Him, to them gave he power to become the sons of God, even to them that believe on His name."*

I could see from this verse that it takes an act of will. We must receive Him to "become sons." In *Revelation* 22:17 (the latter part of verse 17) says: *"And whosoever will, let him take the water of life freely."*

And using *John* 3, Andy explained about Nicodemus, a ruler of the Jews. This religious leader needed to be born again. He needed to be born of water and of Spirit.

At this point in my life in 1965, I had been teaching Sunday school classes and was not unlike Nicodemus. I realized that I was lost and was now looking for answers just as Nicodemus was in his day. This chapter explains that the water birth is the first birth from a mother. By this point in my career, I had delivered countless baby calves and piglets and knew they were born in a water sack. The amniotic sack surrounds the young until birth when it breaks all over the pants of the veterinarian.

John 3:4 (the latter part of verse 4) asks the question: *"Can he enter the second time into his mother's womb, and be born?"*

I am certainly qualified to answer that question: "No way, Bubba!" You will never push one back in after delivery! So, we have established that each of us is born of water. The question that still remains, *"Are you born of the Spirit?"*

Romans 6:11–14 states:

> *"Likewise reckon ye also yourselves to be dead indeed unto sin, but alive unto God through Jesus Christ our*

Lord. Let not sin therefore reign in your mortal body,
that ye should obey it in the lusts thereof. Neither yield
ye your members as instruments of unrighteousness
unto sin: but yield yourselves unto God, as those that
are alive from the dead, and your members as instru-
ments of righteousness unto God. For sin shall not have
dominion over you, for ye are not under the law, but
under grace."

The above verse explains the *real water baptism* and how we
need to reckon ourselves to be dead unto sin but alive until God
through Jesus Christ our Lord. It is a *heart issue* in which we choose
to forego the things of the flesh for the spiritual things of God. It is
not of our own actions or even that of our parents by an act of
baby baptism, but by the grace of God that at an age of accounta-
bility we can be born of the Spirit. How? We first must yield the
inherent sinful nature of our flesh to God. God, in turn, through
His master plan of grace, transforms us back into His spiritual
nature, making us righteous in God's sight. So, why do we want to
give up this sin nature? The answer is found in *Romans* 6:23:

"For the wages of sin is death, but the gift of God is
eternal life through Jesus Christ our Lord."

On one of Andy's visits, he explained *I John* 5:13:

"These things have I written unto you that believe on
the name of the Son of God; that ye may know that ye
have eternal life, and that ye may believe on the name
of the Son of God."

Andy explained that we are to *know* that we are saved and *know* that we are on our way to heaven! I remember that this verse was very important to JoAnne. First, we are to be sure, and, second, we are to believe on the Name (*Jesus*) of the Son of God.

So, how do we yield to or believe on God? It is merely an act of faith by an individual who asks the Lord to transform his or her heart (or, to be born again into God's spiritual nature) and who believes that God will be faithful to perform this transformation according to His promise in the Word of God. This is further explained in *Romans* 3:22–26:

> "*Even the righteousness of God which is by faith of Jesus Christ unto all and upon all them that believe: for there is no difference. For all have sinned, and come short of the glory of God. Being justified freely by his grace through the redemption that is in Christ Jesus. Whom God hath set forth to be a propitiation through faith in his blood, to declare his righteousness for the remission of sins that are past, through the forbearance of God. To declare, I say, at this time his righteousness: that he might be just, and the justifier of him which believeth in Jesus.*"

These biblical principles changed my entire purpose for living. Basically, I was *born of the Spirit*.

About mid-September 1965, I was on my knees and calling out to God. I said, "*Lord, I don't know where I am in my walk with You. I don't want this uncertainty any longer. Please, Jesus, come into my heart and save my soul. I give You my life and promise to follow You. Forgive me my sins, Lord, and save me.*"

That prayer changed my life! I knew I was a changed man, and

God proved it to me, by opening up the scriptures so that I could understand them. JoAnne and I had read the *New Testament* at least five times before this time, but on this night the scriptures became a true part of my life and I could understand how it related to me personally. The bending of my soul toward God that had started those many years ago as a teenager became aligned with God's plan and His will for my life that night. *My soul got bent! This was my turning point! Glory to God!*

JoAnne had a personal encounter with Jesus earlier, but that is her story. Now, praise God, we both were new creations, and we were a new family. God could now teach us and use us like He used Andy, Al, and Jan—and God did just that!

"Friend, do you know where you will spend eternity?" The passage of *1 John* 5:13 referred to above states that you can *know* for sure. If you do not recall anything else from this book other than to seek this answer to the question, then you got the entire purpose of why I chose to write my story. This is the *most important lesson* to be learned. **This key life lesson I learned at that time is** *"In Him (Jesus) was life and the life was the light of men."*

It was this time after my conversion that the Lord reminded me that I had promised to preach the gospel. All those years during school, followed by six years of working as a veterinarian, that promise I had made had never been an issue. Really, it had not bugged me until now!

As you will see, even though God had transformed my heart into a new creature in Him, He still had some fine-tuning to perform on my life. I had been back to work about two days after being saved when I was working some cattle and caught myself saying a swear word. It had been very easy for me to swear while moving cattle or working on livestock of any kind. The Lord said,

"Stop it!" How did He say it? Let me answer with a *Bible* verse, *Ephesians* 3:16:

> *"That He would grant you, according to the riches of His glory, to be strengthened with might by His Spirit in the inner man". [emphasis added]*

That "Stop it!" by the Lord was spoken to *the inner man.* I cannot explain how it works exactly because it is a spiritual contact. I knew it was God, and He meant what He said.

As soon as I was in the truck and alone, I prayed. *"Lord forgive me for taking your name in vain and breaking the 3rd commandment. Help me not to use those words anymore."* Because of this experience, I bought a large gospel sign that was 16 x 22 inches with the following reminder from *Exodus* 20:7:

> *"THOU SHALT NOT TAKE THE NAME OF THE LORD THY GOD IN VAIN: FOR THE LORD WILL NOT HOLD HIM GUILTLESS THAT TAKETH HIS NAME IN VAIN." (emphasis added)*

I hung this scripture verse up in my office and left it up for all these years to remind me that at one time, this sin had control of me. But, thanks be to God, because of Christ it was rooted out and my mouth was cleaned up to be used to praise His Name.

Permit me to say that your problem may be different from mine, but if you will open your heart to God He will speak to your *inner man* and help you solve any problem. This experience helped me a great deal. I recognized how God can communicate with believers. I recognized how *Old Testament* men and women were moved to do certain things by faith as described in *Hebrews* 11.

Turning point? Yes, this was a turning point in our lives. JoAnne and I began to seek out other folks for relationships and fellowship that centered on the things of the Lord. From this point in my life, I wanted to *reach out* to my children, my extended family, my friends and my clients. Our prior pursuits of the things of this world were exchanged for the things of God as a result of being born of the Spirit. Our motivation for our lives had been changed as delineated in *Matthew* 16:26:

> *"For what is a man profited, if he shall gain the whole world, and lose his own soul? Or what shall a man give in exchange for his soul?"*

Do you have a need for a turning point in your life? Sometimes we face a problem that is too big for us to handle by ourselves, and we need help. The Holy Spirit is available to help us. God stands ready with His strength to gently help carry the load or lift the burdens within your life. Over and over in my life, I have felt this nudging and encouragement to move on *in Him*.

The long trip I have been on during my lifetime is difficult to put on paper, but I pray that as you read this, you can relate to some of the situations and see where you have experienced similar blessings and instructions from God in your own circumstances. Maybe a dream, maybe a situation, or maybe a trial and when it was all over, you can say with confidence, *"That was God."*

Jacob and the ladder dream is found in the *Genesis* 28:10–18. *Genesis* 28:17 states:

> *"And he was afraid, and said, How dreadful is this*

*place! This is none other but the house of God, and this
is the gate of heaven."*

Where was Jacob that day? He was traveling and was in a certain place. Perhaps you are at a certain place today? For Jacob, the place was Bethel, but for me it was west central Minnesota. For you, it may be the backyard of *adversity.*

One of the gifts given to believers (those God has redeemed through His grace of salvation) is the gift of *discerning of spirits.* We do it all the time and do not even acknowledge that it is from God. We visit with someone and when we get back in the car we say, *"I don't trust that man."* Or, we say, *"Boy, is he mixed up."* Or we might even say, *"I really felt comfortable with that person and would like to visit with him or her sometime again."*

I recall now that when I was a boy, near the age of ten, I had a vivid dream:

> *"I was at a shore of a lake where the sand was very fine
> and lay as far as the eye could see. Smooth and calm.
> All of a sudden something stirred up the sand and
> made it look rough and ugly, full of ruts and even some
> blood here and there.*
>
> *Next the waves came and washed onto the shore. Wave
> after wave and soon I noticed that the sand was smooth
> and beautiful again."*

My dream stopped there, but even today I can see this severe stirring in the sand and then the calm. Life had dealt some trials, frustrations and heartaches, but with time and the washing of the water of the Word, the beach of my life gets smooth and calm again.

So, what am I trying to say? Basically, there are bumps in the road of life and everything along the way doesn't always go smoothly on this trip, but by taking the Lord along for the journey, He will work through these difficult times for His glory on His timetable.

In the *Bible*, one of the individuals with the most documented set of tribulations was a man called Job. After living through all these tragic events in his life, he describes God's smoothing restoration in his life. It is found in *Job* 42:10–11:

> "And the Lord turned the captivity of Job, when he prayed for his friends: also the Lord gave Job twice as much as he had before. Then came there unto him all his brethren, and all his sisters, and all they that had been of his acquaintance before, and did eat bread with him in his house: and they bemoaned him, and comforted him over all the evil that the Lord had brought upon him: every man also gave him a piece of money, and every one an earring of gold."

I recall an event in the life of one of my former customers. I am thinking of Dennis Keller and his dairy farm. If you recall, he was among one of my first customers after I completed vet school. He had a beautiful place, purebred Holstein cattle with high production, and most importantly, a wonderful family. One day, a tornado came through this farm. When the storm was over, the barn was destroyed and twelve head of these dairy cattle were dead. The balance of the cattle had to be sold to the market. I spoke to Mrs. Dennis Keller in June 2004, and she said that they are grain farmers now! Thanks Dennis for the memories, and may God Bless your family.

The lesson of life I learned from this event was: "*Sometimes things turn to mud!*" We must praise God anyway: like my dream as a boy, sometimes the beach gets messed up and bloody. Trust God during these periods and wait for His gentle waves to make things smooth again.

No matter where you are in your life today, God the Creator has a *plan* that is not contingent on your circumstances. The *plan* is paid for and you are pre-qualified based on Jesus Christ's credit rating. All you have to do is reach out by faith and ask God to transform your heart into His image. I pray that, like I did those nearly forty years ago, you, too, will accept Jesus Christ as your personal savior.

CHAPTER NINE

Minnesota Mentoring Period

We had many *Bible* studies. From fall 1965 until spring 1968, several families met for *Bible* study and prayer 2–5 days a week. Initially, JoAnne and I had continued in our local Lutheran church. However, as we studied the *Bible* and gained new insights into God's Word, I started to share this with my Sunday school class in church. This created doctrinal friction for the pastor as members of my class started to question their beliefs and that of the church with the pastor. One Saturday, our pastor came over to our house to visit with me. He asked that I not come back to the church any more due to doctrinal differences.

As such, JoAnne and I met in the evenings and on Sundays to pray and study God's Word with others families in either our home or those of these other families. Sometimes, it was Andy, JoAnne and myself. At other times, it was Al and Jan and us. And, at other times, it was Paul and JoAnn Bruns, Gordon and Betty Thorstad, JoAnne, and I. On some occasions, there were visitors from Minneapolis or the Shonebergs from Hoffman, Minnesota.

Gil Heegard from Starbuck didn't come but was with us in spirit. This was our schooling and God knew that we needed to mature in Him.

I had read the *Bible* off and on while in college and also in Wheaton. But now, we started having serious, family devotion times. Many of the students at the Morris campus of the University of Minnesota started coming to our home for *Bible* studies. Dave Gandrud, Barbara Gandrud, David Ask, and Lee Turner were among those who attended. They were very musical and helped hold our children's interest in the gospel. I played the guitar well enough to help. Our children liked to sing! We sang a lot of gospel songs and choruses. By now, we had six children: David, Darwin, Kevin, Julie, Jane, and Karen.

David, the oldest, was eleven years old. Our children knew that their parents had changed and were truly a part of the revival. One time we were having lunch in a restaurant and Karen was along. Karen was four years old and not yet in school. The waitress made a comment on how happy we seemed to be. Karen spoke up and said, *"We are a happy family you know."* I am so glad that joy is one of the fruits of the Spirit, as pointed out in *Galatians* 5:22–23:

> *"But the fruit of the Spirit is love, joy, peace, long-suffering, gentleness, goodness, faith, meekness, temperance (or self control): against such there is no law."*

Who in their right mind would not want to eat that fruit?

During this period, JoAnne's dad, Art Jackson, passed away on March 29, 1966. He was buried in the cemetery next to Barsness Lutheran Church. This was the first funeral that my young children had been exposed to. Prior to Art's passing, JoAnne and I were able to have some meaningful time of fellowship with Art before his surgery and subsequent medical complications from his stay in the hospital.

As we continued down this path, things started happening that we did not yet understand. One Sunday morning during *Bible* study, one teenage girl, Nancy, began to cry. We asked, *"What's wrong, Nancy?"*

Nancy answered, *"I don't know, but I feel I need Jesus. I want to get saved."* Outside my own conversion, I had never seen anything like this. *"What do we do?"* Mrs. Bruns knew what was happening and helped her with the *Sinner's Prayer:*

> *"Lord, I am a sinner and am sorry for my sins. I confess them to you now Lord. Lord God, forgive me for my sins and come into my heart. Save me! And set me free from sin, death and the power of the devil. Help me to live for you. In Jesus' Name. Amen."*

After the prayer, Nancy became so happy and excited about what Gad had just done in her life. We would hear all of the children pray this prayer as we moved along during the next several years. One night at the Bruns home, about seven miles north of Morris, Minnesota, we were studying about the power of Satan as revealed in scriptures. We saw how Christ proclaimed victory over Satan when He died on the Cross of Calvary and thus defeated Satan. This home was a two-story home and had heat vents in the ceiling. At about 10 P.M., we heard loud crying and three teenage boys came downstairs. They wanted to be saved. They had been laying upstairs by the grate listening to the *Bible* study and realized they needed God's forgiveness in their respective lives. The Holy Spirit is not impeded by grates in the ceiling but reaches into even the tiny rooms of our heart if we will let Him. What a Savior! What a Christ!

So, what was going on in these lives? We see in *Titus* 3:5 that the answer is *regeneration* or spiritual birth:

> *"Not by works of righteousness which we have done, but according to His mercy He saved us, by the washing of regeneration, and renewing of the Holy Ghost."*

The concept of regeneration is further explained in the *Full Life Study Bible* with several of its key points:

~ *"Regeneration is a re-creating and transformation of the person by God the Holy Spirit. Through this process eternal life from God Himself is imparted to the believer, and he becomes a child of God. He no longer conforms to this world, but is now created after God 'in righteousness and true holiness'."*

~ *"Regeneration is necessary because apart from Christ, all people, by their inherent natures, are sinners, incapable of obeying and pleasing God."*

~ *"Regeneration comes to those who repent of their sin, turn to God, and place personal faith in Jesus Christ as Lord and Savior."*

~ *"Regeneration involves a transition from an old life of sin to a new life of obedience to Jesus Christ. The one who is truly born again is set free from the bondage of sin and receives a spiritual desire and disposition to obey God and follow the leading of the Spirit. Those born again live righteous lives, love other believers, avoid a life of sin, and do not love the world."*

The regeneration concept is summarized by *The Machintosh Treasury*:

"In a word, then, regeneration is God's own work, from first to last. God is the Operator; man is the happy, privileged subject. His co-operation is not sought in a work which must ever bear the impress of one almighty hand. God was alone in creation, alone in redemption, and He must be alone in the mysterious and glories work of regeneration."

Obviously, besides this spiritual awakening transforming my life, I continued to practice veterinarian medicine on a daily basis. I remember one call. But, first a little background.

In 1965, Minnesota and many other states were still fighting brucellosis in cattle. Some states are brucellosis free now, some are not. Al and I did brucellosis testing at the state's expense during those years and as such, often worked with brucellosis positive herds.

One morning, I stood looking at an aborted, dead, rotten calf at about four gestational months. A full term calf is carried by the mother for nine months. This calf was lying under a barbed wire fence in hot summer sun and smelled pretty bad. The owner and I discussed brucellosis and planned to test the herd on a certain date. Abortion at three to four months gestation is common with brucellosis and is also the time when other cattle in the herd are exposed to the disease.

While in earnest prayer by myself one evening, I asked God to show me who I was in His kingdom's work? Immediately, God showed me that aborted fetus under the fence line and spoke to my *inner man* and said, *"That's you."* As a grown man, I cried out loud at the shameful image of who I was in God's eye without Christ. When I regained my composure, I told God that was a real mess and worthless, good for nothing! If that is me, what value am I to the kingdom of God? The Lord reminded me that He makes things out of nothing. Glory to God! Yes, people make things out of raw materials or others things, but God makes and creates from nothing. *Romans* 3:9–18 highlights the true condition of man without God's cleansing power:

> *"What then? Are we better than they? No, in no wise: for we have before proved both Jews and Gentiles, that they are all under sin. As it is written, there is none righteous, no, not one. There is none that understandeth, there is none that seeketh after God. They are all gone out of the way, they are together become unprofitable; there is none that doeth good, no, not one. Their throat is an open sepulchre; with their tongues they have used deceit; the poison of asps is under their lips. Whose mouth is full of cursing and bitterness. Their feet are swift to shed blood. Destruction and misery are in their ways. And the way of peace have they not known. There is no fear of God before their eyes."*

H. A. Ironside, in his book, *Romans: Inside Commentaries*, further lays out the true case against man along with God's justification of man by describing *Romans* as "*The Epistle of the **Forum:**"*

> *"In this letter (book of Romans) the sinner is brought into the court room, the **forum**, the place of judgment, and shown to be utterly guilty and undone. But through the work of Christ a righteous basis has been laid, upon which he can be justified from every charge. Nor does God stop here, but He openly acknowledges the believing sinner as His own son,*

*making him a citizen of a favored race, and owning
him as His heir. Thus, the challenge can be hurled at
all objectors, 'What shall we then say to these things?
If God be for us, what can be against us?' Every voice
is silenced, for 'It is God that justifies,' and this not at
the expense of righteousness, but in full accord with
His righteousness."*

By 1966, there was a *small town stir* in Morris, Minnesota. Clicking of teeth as people wondered what happened to these guys. Some of this got back to us, and I am sure much is left to be told. Andy Joranger drove a Dodge. Al and myself both drove Dodge trucks at the time. People in town were calling us the *Dodge Boys*. Glory! Ken Varnum and his wife, Marilyn, started listening to Andy also about this time. They were wonderfully saved and have been a blessing to JoAnne and me for years. We often go to their home for *Bible* study and fellowship while visiting back in Minnesota. Al and Jan Trumble have been faithful there and meet each week with Varnums and several new families.

That brings me to faithfulness. God is faithful, but man can back out or run from God. The best comments I know of for these thoughts are from a little book called *Statement of Faith and Discipline for Original Free Will Baptists of North Carolina*. The following is from a 1955 revision of the treatise of faith and government for the original Free Will Baptists of North Carolina (Chapter XIII: **Perseverance of the Saints**):

> *"There are strong grounds to hope that the truly regenerate will persevere unto the end, and be saved, through the power of divine grace which is pledged for their support; but their future obedience and final salvation are*

*neither determined nor certain, since through infirmity
and manifold temptations they are in danger of falling;
and they ought therefore to watch and pray, lest they
make shipwreck of their faith and be lost."*

All of those folks whom I have spoken about previously, that were involved in the revival that occurred in Morris, Minnesota, stand before God on their own. *Philippians* 2:12 tells us:

*"Wherefore, my beloved, as ye have always obeyed, not
as in my presence only, but now much more in my
absence, work out your own salvation with fear and
trembling."*

By outside appearances, it would seem that not all seed was sown on good soil, some of those who studied with us endured but for a while. I will let God be the judge and say to brethren, be careful and work out your own salvation with fear and trembling. Godly fear!

Some folks will be offended at me for speaking and writing like this. But why? We can speak of what the children played and said, what the weather is going to do, how to shop for groceries and much more; but, are we to keep to ourselves the most important decision of our lives, our *eternal destiny*? We found this out as I started witnessing about Christ and His precious Word. Some clients did not want me to come to their place anymore because I gave them a gospel tract. Some accepted the tracts and were not offended. Many said they had a church home and did not want to talk about it.

At first, I thought everyone would be glad to talk about the things of God. But then I realized that some believed Jesus and some rejected Him. The real church that became a part of our lives is found in *Hebrews* 12:22–24:

> *"But ye are come unto mount Zion, and unto the city of the living God, the heavenly Jerusalem, and to an innumerable company of angels, to the general assembly and church of the first-born, which are written in heaven, and to God the Judge of all, and to spirits of just men made perfect, and to Jesus the mediator of the new covenant, and to the blood of sprinkling, that speaketh better things than that of Abel."*

Hebrews 12:28 goes on to say:

> *"Wherefore we receiving a kingdom which cannot be moved, let us have grace, whereby we may serve God acceptably with reverence and godly fear."*

And, *Revelation* 1:6 states:

> *"And hath made us kings and priests unto God and His Father; to Him be glory and dominion for ever and ever. Amen."*

That is real church!

Jim Keep was a dairy farmer at Herman, Minnesota. He always accepted gospel tracts when I left his place after treating his livestock. Jim was missing an arm from a corn-picker accident and for this reason often had teenagers helping with the dairy. I gave them gospel tracts, too. One night while at a *Bible* study at the Bruns' place, I received a call to treat a milk fever cow in Herman,

Minnesota. It was my evening on duty, so off I drove. Before leaving the *Bible* study, however, someone mentioned Jim Keep. They said, *"Jim is sick with a bad heart and was going to have heart surgery on Monday morning."*

It was a Saturday night and there was a bad snowstorm. When I finished treating the cow for milk fever, it was already 1:30 A.M. The Lord spoke to my *inner man* and told me to go see Jim! Driving was very slow due to the snow; I drove into Jim's driveway at 2:20 A.M. *"This must be foolish,"* I told God, but then I noticed the light was on in the kitchen. I knocked on the door and Jim came to the door and said, *"Come in. I was expecting you."*

I started by asking Jim, *"Did you ever read any of those gospel tracts I left with you?"*

"Yes," he said, *"everyone of them."* We studied the Word together for over an hour that night and Jim accepted Jesus as his personal Savior and Lord. I asked Jesus to heal Jim's physical heart and his *inner man* — and Jesus did! I have now lost contact with Jim, but five years later he still had not had surgery.

Mark 16:15–20 speaks about the signs that should follow them that believe. The last part of verses 13 and 14 say:

> *"In my name shall they cast out devils; they shall speak with new tongues.... they shall lay hands on the sick, and they shall recover."*

I knew God was there that night, and I learned more about how to be tuned in to the leading of the Spirit.

I Thessalonians 5:23 says:

> *"And the very God of peace sanctify you wholly; and I pray God your whole spirit and soul and body be pre-*

served blameless unto the coming of our Lord Jesus Christ."

You and I are three parts: body, soul, and spirit. No! No! That is backwards. We are really spirit, soul, and body—spirit first. You and I are spirit beings first! Help us, oh God, to be tuned into your Holy Spirit who can guide us into all truth as articulated in *John* 16:13.

JoAnne and I went to an Oral Roberts meeting in the summer of 1966 at Moline, Illinois. We wanted to learn more about the Holy Ghost. However, everything was not pleasant between my folks and us during this time. As I have already discussed, they were devoted Lutherans and did not like having their faith questioned or challenged. After JoAnne and I had returned home from this Oral Roberts meeting, we invited my folks over for dinner. I mentioned that we had gone to the meeting. Dad got very angry and told Mom he was going home! If she wanted to go along, she had to leave right away! *They left.*

In hindsight, this response was predictable from Dad. Based on research articulated in the book *Profiles of Lutherans in the USA,* the researchers made the case that *"Being Lutheran . . . is virtually a family affair."* The researchers go on to layout the statistics that 90 percent of Lutherans are family-undergirded: 75-percent have been raised from childhood as Lutherans and another 15-percent as the result of a marriage relationship. My new spiritual path was at odds with my family's religious heritage. You will see later in the book, these things worked out over time, and later Dad had our auction sale before we headed to Texas.

During summer 1967, we spent a week with Gerald Derstine Ministries at Strawberry Lake, Minnesota. We still wanted to know more about the Holy Ghost and healing. We stayed in a one-room cabin. It was like a *Bible* camp. We had three services a day and a little time in the afternoon for the children to swim. After this meeting, I was convinced that I needed to be re-baptized by immersion. Andy's original dart of *"There is nothing to baby baptism"* was clearly backed up by the scriptures as I studied the doctrinal aspects of this biblical practice.

Acts 8, talks about Philip preaching to the Eunuch who asks about being baptized by immersion. *Acts* 8:36–38 describes the scene. Verse 36 says:

> *"And as they went on their way, they came unto a certain water; and the eunuch said, See, here is water; what doth hinder me to be baptized?"*

Then, in verse 37, Philip responds:

> *"And Philip said, If thou believest with all thine heart, thou mayest. And he answered and said, I believe that Jesus Christ is the Son of God."*

The eunuch's action follows in verse 38:

> *"And he commanded the chariot to stand still; and they went down both into the water, both Philip and the eunuch; and he baptized him."*

They had a baptismal service at the camp, but I knew many of those that were meeting with us at Morris did not believe we needed to be baptized again. *I Corinthians* 8 explains the reason I knew it was not the appropriate time for me to be baptized. I will not try to show you what I see in this chapter, but it does tell us to watch out for our brothers.

Several months later, we met at the Bruns' home and a sermon was given by a brother from Minneapolis. The message was baptism the *Bible* way. *Acts* 8 was discussed and immersion was presented as the *Bible* mode for this sacrament. Baby baptism was touched on also, *but because a baby can't believe it was dismissed.* Again, looking in *Acts* 8:37, Philip stated:

> "*If thou believest with all thine heart, thou mayest (be baptized).*"

Romans 6 really tells the story on baptism. Verse 11 states:

> "*Likewise reckon ye also yourselves to be dead indeed unto sin, but alive unto God through Jesus Christ our Lord.*"

We identify ourselves with Jesus's death when we go under the water. Going back to verse 4:

> "*Therefore we are buried with Him by baptism into death: that like as Christ was raised up from the dead by the glory of the Father, even so we also should walk in newness of life.*"

And then verse 5:

> "*For if we have been planted together in the likeness of*

His death, we shall be also in the likeness of his resur-
rection."

This is a precious truth because the old, sinful man is left in
the water and is washed into the Gulf of Mexico. The new creature, the new man, is resurrected with Christ and begins to live a
new life. *Now this does not happen at baptism, but at the new*
birth. The baptism helps us to see what happened in the new birth,
and we identify ourselves with this great work of Christ. Glory!

Romans 6:1–2 states:

> *"What shall we say, then? Shall we continue in sin, that*
> *grace may abound? God forbid. How shall we, that are*
> *dead to sin, live any longer therein?"*

We stop living in sin because the old man is dead and we can
allow the new man to grow in grace and knowledge of Christ.
Note that this does not occur at death of body as is commonly
thought, but like it says in *Romans* 6:11:

> *"Likewise reckon ye also yourselves to be dead indeed*
> *unto sin, but alive unto God through Jesus Christ our*
> *Lord."*

By faith the sinful man dies and by faith the new Christian
becomes alive spiritually. This truth is also presented in
II Corinthians 5:21:

> *"For he hath made him to be sin for us, who knew no sin;*
> *that we might be made the righteousness of God in him."*

These truths become a part of my life and I now prayed, *"Thank you Lord for forgiving all my sins"* instead of, *"Lord, forgive me wherein I have failed and sinned today."* Some will say that this is boasting, but I am not righteous because of what I have done, but because of what **He has done. Glory!**

Well, when the brother from Minneapolis finished his sermon with a call to baptism that evening, I jumped to my feet and asked to be baptized at Pomme De Terre Lake the next morning. *"All those that want to join this man tomorrow, please stand,"* said the preacher. I believe eight stood, and we were baptized the following morning, which happened to be a Sunday.

One that watched that morning was Andy Joranger, the man that helped me and many others find Christ. He had not been baptized by immersion either, but realized that morning that this was of the Lord. He was later baptized also.

This baptismal service caused a split in the Morris group as we expected, but I understand that later, others were obedient to this teaching and were also baptized. I would like to emphasize that *Romans* 6 is the key to understanding this sacrament. That chapter has been a real blessing and a growth chapter for me. Other passages from the scriptures to study on baptism include: *Matthew* 3:13–17, *Matthew* 28:18–20, and *Mark* 16:16.

In some of the other *Bible* studies, we examined other doctrinal beliefs such as the purpose of the Lord's Supper (communion) and the Law (the Ten Commandments). The Lord's Supper is described in four passages: *Matthew* 26:26–29, *Mark* 14:22–25, *Luke* 22:15–20, and *I Corinthians* 11:23–25. The purpose of the Law was discussed in that first *Bible* discussion I had with Andy Joranger while eating ice cream at Al and Jan Trumble's house.

I have made several comments about the *inner man* and the leading of the Spirit and would like to review the scriptures that explain this biblical concept. This is a spiritual truth and needs to be understood.

In *Acts* 8, we can look again at a man of God, Philip. He is at a revival meeting in Samaria and the Angel of the Lord speaks to him in verse 29:

> *"Then the Spirit said until Philip, Go near and join thyself to this chariot."*

Notice how Philip was lead to teach this one man, the Ethiopian eunuch. I first heard this sermon preached by John McIver from Lowry, Minnesota. He emphasized that Philip preached unto Him, Jesus. What a beautiful message and teaching. Please read it again from the *Bible*.

Paul was also led by the Spirit as Philip had been. We can see this in *Acts* 16:9–10. Through a vision, Paul was called to a new area, named Macedonia:

> *"And after he had seen the vision, immediately we endeavored to go into Macedonia, assuredly gathering that the Lord had called us for to preach the gospel unto them."*

And Abraham was led by the Spirit to go to a new land that God would later show him. Many biblical scholars believe the events recorded in *Acts* are ongoing—that *"it won't be over until it is over."*

The above discussion of God's leading is very practical and personal to me. God helped me in my veterinary work. One day I received a call about 1,000 calves (about 550 lb. feeders) that were coughing and sick for the second time. I had treated these calves with a sulfa drug we put in their water two weeks earlier, at a price of about $1,200. On the way to the call, I told God we were in trouble and there was no way we could treat 1,000 calves individually. I knew the owner was upset, and I asked God what I should do. God spoke to my heart and told me to put them back on sulfa the second time. It would be okay. After checking the calves with temperatures of 104–106°F, I explained to the owner that we were going to repeat the same treatment. The owner didn't think it would work but agreed to the plan. These calves responded and grew well in the feedlot. Thanks be to God!

One day when driving the veterinary truck to a call, I had a severe, sharp pain my in chest. I called out really loudly *"Jesus, Jesus!"* The pain stopped and never came back.

One of my uncles, William Dalager died. JoAnne and I went to the funeral. William had twelve children (my cousins) who were all present, of course. At the service, the Lord spoke to my *inner man* and said one of these children is hungry for God! There was a time for visiting following the service, so I started searching for the hungry one. Some had heard that Hans Peterson was crazy about religion and did not want to visit with me. Then I spoke to my namesake (cousin Hans Dalager), and he wanted to know about death and Christ. We visited for a while and he promised to come to Morris for *Bible* study and prayer. Hans and Jeanne Dalager and their two children came often for prayer. Hans had Hodgkin's disease at the time and died about a year later in a Minneapolis hospital. This was a shock to me because we had prayed so much that God would heal his body. Hans's death made a big impact on us as a family. God chose not to heal Hans and called him home.

One Friday on my day off, I went with Gill Heegard from Starbuck to the jails in Benson, Minnesota and Wilmer,

Minnesota. He visited every week to preach to the jail inmates, sing and just show them someone cared about them. It was a real blessing! The prisoners were real people! They didn't have horns and not one of them had ever done anything wrong! When we left, Gil said, *"Don't you come back to go with me; you go find some other jail and preach and teach."* Maybe I'm not ready for this, I thought.

On another day, I prayed to God for guidance about this jail work. We had noticed as we studied God's Word that there was a purpose for our lives, and we wanted to serve God—this was not because we had to do so, but because we wanted to do so.

Lord, I am afraid to visit the inmates in the jail. How can you assure me of your help and protection? *"Open the Bible and read,"* so I opened my *Bible* to *I John* 3:20–21:

> *"For if our heart condemn us, God is greater than our heart, and knoweth all things. Beloved, if our heart condemn us not, then have we confidence toward God."*

Did my heart condemn me? I answered, *"No, Lord, I trust you."* If my heart did not condemn me, I could act in confidence that He would know where I was and would work with me. *"Okay, God."* The next Thursday I started a jail service at Whapeton, South Dakota and in Fergus Falls, Minnesota. The prison officials were very polite and welcomed me. The jail in Whapeton had catwalks, so I could speak to them through the bars. Not so in Fergus Falls. They opened the door and put me in with the prisoners.

That first service at the Fergus Falls jail was a real education. There were six inmates, mostly young adults and teenagers. The biggest one told me I had no business there and that he was going to push me through the bars. I told him to sit down and listen! *"God has a message for you and this is it."* With that, I presented the gospel and left. The next week the same fellow said, *"Come on in. I tested you last week and you passed the test."* That week we made real progress. The man agreed to read the *New Testament* I had brought during the week. Throughout my jail ministry, I would supply *New Testaments* to anyone in the jail that would accept the Word.

Several weeks later, four men in the Fergus Falls jail cell prayed for salvation. One of these boys said, *"I felt that."* He was young and simple, and God wanted him to know it was real. Thanks be to God!

There was one man at Whapeton that I remember well. I will call him "A. F." The first three or four times I visited him, he told me I could sing, but he would not listen to me preach. So, we sang choruses and visited a little and that was it. During this time, I read a newspaper account of his crime. A. F. set a man's clothes on fire so that he could rob him. This guy was a bad dude. When I came in on the fifth week, A. F. wanted to know how he could be forgiven and find peace. He found Christ that week. When I returned again the next week, A. F. had made bail and was gone. I got in my truck and complained in prayer and told God that A. F. needed to be encouraged and spoken to some more before his trial. I was having this mental conversation with God while driving from Fergus Falls to Breckenridge. There was a roadblock due to construction and traffic was completely stopped. A. F. was riding in the car ahead of me and recognized me. He got out of the car and came back to visit with me. He spent time in Stillwater Prison and wrote to me twice while there. I trust to see him in heaven someday; maybe we can sing some choruses together. But, I won't preach!

For about four weeks I had services at a retirement home in Hoffman, Minnesota. At the end of the 4th week, I was asked not to return. I was told that some of the folks were upset after the services. I was not the right denomination or religion for the home's administrator. I found out later that a public address system monitored every room and one lady had confided in me about some of the problems she was having with the retirement home.

While holding a service on one of those weeks, a lady in a wheelchair seemed to be struggling to get closer and closer to the *Bible* that I had opened and was referring to during the *Bible* study. When she finally was able to reach it, she slammed it shut and then relaxed in her chair. When I re-opened it, she became very agitated again until the *Bible* was closed. There was an evil spirit working in that situation. As described in *Galatians* 5:16–25, old or young, the spirit fights the flesh!

The retirement home was a depressing place to me and my hat is off to anyone who can minister in these circumstances. I was convinced that my calling was not to go to retirement or rest homes.

During spring 1968, we attended a week of teaching and ministry at Cokoto, Minnesota. There was still snow on the ground. The Missionary Revival Crusade from Laredo, Texas was having their annual conference when we attended. JoAnne and the children were with me and we enjoyed the singing and fellowship of missionaries. Several of these new missionary families attending were soon headed to Mexico. These meetings taught us more about the things of God.

A missionary lady, Bernice Oser, was one of the speakers. Her home and mission field was Saltillo, Mexico. Bernice was alone in that area and pleaded for men to come and help in the mission field. Bernice was probably sixty years old at the time and weary from the load. To reach the Mexico men, she felt she needed a *man's voice*. This sermon tugged at my heart, but I pushed it aside. Daniel Ost, the founder and president of Missionary Revival Crusade, was also there and preached several times, telling about Mexico and the desire they shared to get the gospel to all the people of Mexico. We learned that Brother Ost would be preaching at Starbuck, Minnesota on the next Friday night, and because this was close to home we planned to attend.

On that Friday, while home for lunch, I said to JoAnne, *"What would constitute a call to the mission field? If an angel came into this room and said, 'Go,' would we go?"*

"Oh yes," JoAnne said, *"we would go."*

*"Then, if a **man of God** said we were to go to the mission field, would we go?"*

"Oh yes," JoAnne answered, *"we would go then also."* We were interrupted by the children and nothing more was said.

That evening at Starbuck we arrived at the meeting early and were met by Brothers Gil Heegard and Danny Ost. Danny picked up a guitar and began to play and sing. He made up verse after verse telling how Hans Peterson was needed for the mission work in Mexico. In light of what JoAnne and I had discussed at noon that day, this was a real shock! Here was a **man of God** telling us to go to the mission field and even telling us where to go! After Danny preached that night, I told the group of about twenty people gathered there what had happened that day. I told them we would plan to go as soon as possible because we felt called of the Lord. The men laid hands on me that evening and prayed God's blessing on our preparation to begin our new ministry.

There were many unanswered questions, but the next day I told Al Trumble, my partner, that we would be leaving. I worked until the first of June and began preparations to move our family to Mexico. JoAnne was pregnant with our 7th child, so we made our plans around that upcoming event. Sandra would be born in Morris, Minnesota, and then we would travel.

The last day that I worked in Morris, I used my cattle chute at a ranch south of town. When we were done with the cattle, the farmer asked about the rumor that we were moving. I told him I was working my last day, and he wished me well. *"How about the cattle chute?"* I said, *"Do you want to buy it from me?"* He said he would, and Leonard Wulf gave me my asking price. He said it would help me with the move.

We had seen God's hand on our family during the last couple of years as He mentored us, but from the time we made this decision to follow what we believed was His plan for us, we really saw Him move. We want God to receive all the glory and praise. And, as I recount the next four months of how we got to the mission field, I pray that you, the reader, will rejoice with us at this undeniable demonstration of God's grace.

In thinking of this period in my life, I want to give a special thanks to Andy Joranger and Al and Jan Trumble for following the instructions in the Word to reach others for Christ. I want to thank many others that have helped me in my walk with the Lord. Thanks to the Thorstad, Bruns, Varnum, Mecklenberg, McIver, Johnson, and Hegard families, plus David Gandrud, Danny Ost, Curtis Peterson, and the students from the University of Minnesota in Morris that came by to study. Mainly, thanks to Jesus for He has been closer than a brother.

The life lesson I learned from this period of my life was: *"As we walk out in faith to follow God, His Spirit provides direction in very practical ways as He guides us toward His plan for our lives, as we yield to His path for our life."*

CHAPTER TEN

South Texas Mission Field Years

On June 5, 1968, Robert Kennedy was shot and killed at the Ambassador Hotel in Los Angeles. That announcement on the radio came the same day I was driving to see Mexico for the first time. That trip from Morris, Minnesota to Laredo, Texas was about 1,500 miles. I drove long hours and was at the headquarters of the Missionary Revival Crusade at Laredo about 4:00 P.M. on June 6. I expected this to be a real spiritual treat and was looking forward to devotions that evening with a few missionaries. One missionary did come by shortly after I did and had a motorcycle problem. We worked together to fix the problem and the house director showed me a small room where I could spend the night. The mosquitoes were just a little smaller than buzzards, and it was hot—*TEXAS HOT!*

The next morning, I left early and drove to Saltillo, Mexico to meet and help Bernice Oser. You will recall she spoke at Cokoto Convention and needed a man's help. Well, here comes the help! When I stopped for breakfast in Monterey that morning, I ate eggs for breakfast. I didn't want eggs, but the only Spanish words I knew were *por favor* (please) and *juevos* (eggs), so that's what I ordered.

Bernice was living in a small village close to Saltillo called Belle Union. It was beautiful there; mountains to one side and a waterfall coming out of the rocks on the other side, flowing into a river. The people living in the pueblo used this river for all of their water needs, including laundry and swimming, and the dogs and pigs walked around in the running water as well.

Bernice received me graciously and politely and began to help me with the vowels of the Spanish language. I really thought that Spanish would be easily learned. I would work on it maybe for about thirty days, and bingo, I would know the language. I slept in the truck for three nights and helped around the place. Bernice took me into Saltillo one day for a Mexican meal. The last day I was there, Bernice hired a cement laborer to put a cement floor in her home. This man's name was Estachio Soto, and he was about fifty years old. Estachio had twelve children, and I believe most of them were girls, as I recall.

While waiting for the cement to set, Bernice interpreted for me so I could testify and share the gospel with Estachio. He listened very intently, and I gave him the only Spanish *Bible* that I had brought along. He promised to come to the services at the mission on the following Sunday.

Leaving Saltillo, I arrived in Laredo and stayed in a motel. That night, I did some real praying. *"God you have made a big mistake. I cannot communicate with these people. The language is a roadblock for me."* I complained long and hard, and I told God that it was a big mistake. Gil Heegard had told me about Eagle Pass, Texas and how they had handed out tracts in Spanish and English to the people who crossed the bridge there. They usually went to

Eagle Pass during the winter months to do this mission work. *"God, I am going to go to Eagle Pass tomorrow and look at the town, then I will just head home."* I guess I was making a threat of sorts, but God was listening!

In Eagle Pass, I went first to the Chamber of Commerce and asked if there was a veterinarian in town. *"No! We had one, but two months ago he was called back to the U.S. Reserves and the closest vet now is in Crystal City, 45 miles away."* I thanked the lady for the information and thanked God for answering prayer. I also told the lady I was a veterinarian and would be moving to Eagle Pass as soon as I could.

I called JoAnne and told her we would be moving to Eagle Pass, Texas and that once again I was self-employed. JoAnne said, *"Where is Eagle Pass, Texas?"*

On the trip back to Morris, I talked to God a lot. *"Lord, give JoAnne a healthy baby and an easy delivery."* I prayed that prayer a lot from 1953 to 1971. I am not real sure about the second part of the prayer, but God answered the first part every time. Thanks, God!

My prayers continued, *"Lord, what kind of work? What kind of real mission work will I be doing in Eagle Pass? Lord, some are saying I am crazy for dragging my family to the Mexico border! Lord, help me to know I am on the right road. Lord, I cannot work my way to heaven, so help me to know I am in Your will."* I had questions and more questions—so I drove and prayed.

Then I realized I was lost! I was on the Lewis and Clark Trail. After making a wrong turn by Kansas City, Kansas, I needed to stop and read the map. There was a place to turn off, a big entrance, and pulling over to check the map I saw this large structure. I looked right up at the gate of Leavenworth Prison, in Leavenworth, Kansas. The Lord spoke to my *inner man* and said,

"You will be doing jail work at Eagle Pass and these men need the Word in their hands. Give them the Bible in their own language." After finding my way out of Kansas, I headed home, thanking and praising God as I went.

Arriving back home in Morris, there was a letter from Bernice Oser from Saltillo, Mexico. Her letter told that Estachio Soto had attended services with his family that Sunday, and he wanted to help her with the mission work. God gave her the man she needed to help in her ministry—it was not me, it was Estachio Soto. Some of his children played the guitar and would help with the singing. I thanked God for this letter because it confirmed that I was to help supply *Bibles* to Mexico. If one *Bible* could move Estachio and answer the prayer need of a seasoned missionary, think how 100 or 1,000 *Bibles* would be used to encourage men to seek God.

Getting a letter off to become licensed in Texas was a priority. I was told that Texas had reciprocity with South Dakota, but I had to prove I worked some in that state. Because my first practice had been near the South Dakota state line in Wheaton, Minnesota, I had worked and vaccinated calves in Rosholt, South Dakota and was able to prove that I had indeed practiced in South Dakota. I was told I would need to take a practical exam in College Station, Texas and personally meet with the Board of Veterinary Medical Examiners to get a license. This test was scheduled for the first part of August 1968.

Our 7th child, Sandra Jean was born July 2, 1968. I was at home talking to Andy when the phone rang, and JoAnne informed me Sandra was here and everything was okay. I missed some of those births, but JoAnne was there for every one. Praise the Lord!

Before we could leave for Eagle Pass, we needed to sell most of our possessions in Minnesota. I decided to have an auction sale, and it was scheduled for Wednesday, July 24, 1968. By coincidence, this was Julie's (my oldest daughter) birthday. We had posters made to advertise the event, and I was busy tacking them up around town and in surrounding areas. At a small gas station in Morris, I had just tacked up a poster when a stranger said to me, *"Where are you going?"*

"I am going to Mexico to share the gospel with those in jail and get Bibles into Mexico," I said. He extended his hand and introduced himself. *"I am Bill Chapman, President of the World Home Bible League in Chicago, Illinois. I planned to get gas down the road, but the Spirit said for me to come to this station. This man,"* he continued, and pointing to a tall gentleman standing next to him, *"is Chester Schemper."* We shook hands and he told me that Chester was the head of Latin American *Bible* distribution for Spanish speaking countries of South America. Wow!

Mr. Chapman said, *"We are pleased to meet you, and here is my card. We will send you the first box of Bibles free to get you started in Bible distribution there at the border."* After we were settled in at Eagle Pass, I wrote for the free box of *Bibles,* and they were sent immediately. God was truly guiding our steps.

JoAnne stayed at the hospital about three days and at homecoming, the older children were very excited. They told the neighbors to come and see the new baby. One family that just had to see this new baby was Al and Fran Johnson. They lived across the street from us and were new to the neighborhood. They had two girls and Al was a Professor at University of Minnesota, Morris. Al was working on his thesis for a Ph.D. He told me his subject was the *Spirit of Music* because he was a music major. I laughed and said, *"Which spirit? There are only two. The Spirit of God or the spirit of devil?"* Al was taken back by this statement and wanted me to explain. We discussed the scriptures at length, and he said he needed this *Spirit of God* to control him and to help him with his family and life. Al accepted Christ in the next three weeks or so and became a powerhouse for God over the years that followed. Ye shall receive power when the Holy Spirit comes upon you as explained in *Acts* 1:8:

> "*But ye shall receive power, after that the Holy Ghost is come upon you; and ye shall be witnesses unto me both in Jerusalem, and in all Judea, and in Samaria, and unto the uttermost part of the earth.*"

Al and Fran were a real blessing, seeing us off at 4 A.M. the day we left. They had two daughters when we moved, Marsha and Kristen, and later had a son, Stephan. Al and Fran live in Brainerd, Minnesota. Al and Fran sent money many times to help purchase Spanish *Bibles* to send into Mexico. Thanks Al and Fran. God bless you real good.

The day of the auction sale arrived and my dad was the auctioneer. Dad was the best auctioneer in the world and that day was no exception. A piano we had purchased for $25 sold for $200. Many items sold for more than they were worth.

At suppertime, one of our daughters had a sack of money! I won't say who it was, but her birthday happened to coincide with the date of the sale. *"Where did you get the money?"* Well, as the story unfolded, she really felt bad that she had to part with her bicycle, especially on her birthday! She had told this story to many attending the auction that day, and each one had helped her celebrate her birthday with the offering!

In June, I purchased an aluminum trailer house that was 40-feet long and 8-feet wide. It needed much repair, like new bathroom, paint, and new floors. After the sale, we moved into the trailer home and would live in it until the first part of October 1968. I paid $900 for the new home and for the next few months, we would be wall-to-wall people. *(I ended up selling this trailer in 1971 to some folks from Del Rio, Texas for $3,000.)*

So, at 4 A.M., we said goodbye to our neighbors next door, the Johnson's, and started south. My second son, Darwin was with me and Sandy (the dog) in my veterinarian pickup pulling the trailer. Darwin was riding with me because he had broken his arm in a little league baseball game just prior to our moving. JoAnne and the rest of the children were in a station wagon following me. About three miles south of Morris, the trailer began to sway uncontrollably from side to side. I was able to stop the unstable rig, and we knew two things: God had protected us and we needed something to stop the swaying before we could go much further.

We drove very slowly until we made it to Montevideo, Minnesota, and looked for a trailer expert. The guy said we needed a sway bar. He installed it for us, and it proved to be a challenge to herd that trailer to Texas, but that sway bar helped a lot. When we went through Oklahoma, I-35 was 2-way traffic. Going up those big hills by Sulfur Springs, there were many cars behind us until we came to the top where I could pull off to the side and let them by.

We stopped at Belton Dam, Texas and parked the trailer at a trailer court. The family stayed there and I went on to College Station to take the practical exam and meet with the Board of Medical Examiners to try to get a license to practice veterinary medicine in Texas. Since I was not sent by a mission board with economic support arranged, my livelihood was tied to the outcome of this exam and meeting. The Examiners questioned me, *"Why come to Texas?"* They could not understand about mission work and *Bibles*, but gave me a license to practice in Texas. It is dated August 7, 1968. Thanks, Texas! I am a Texan by examination!

We drove through San Antonio the same week it was host to the World's Fair. *"Yes, your mother drove the car all the way kids, believe it or not, and has been helping me drive ever since."* In one part of San Antonio, I ended up in the left hand lane and could not get over due to the traffic. Pretty soon, a police car had his lights on and was following me. The traffic gave him and me room, and I pulled to the right medium and stopped. JoAnne followed me close behind because she was afraid of losing me. *"Well,"* the cop said, *"you need to stay right." "Yes sir, and thanks so much for helping me over. The traffic would not let me go right."* He escorted me down I-35 for a while and then waved me on.

Highway 57 toward Eagle Pass, Texas was like a desert, with a lot of dried-up sage. I didn't dare stop for fear JoAnne would turn around and go back to Minnesota. But, she didn't! We really have it for one another! The trip down this long stretch of road on that August day of 1968 has almost reached legendary status with the kids, how Dad did not dare stop the truck for fear that Mom would make us all go back to Minnesota when she saw the countryside that scorching hot day! It is a topic of discussion during nearly every family reunion, even these many years later.

God gets the credit for a safe trip, and we arrived in Eagle Pass, Texas.

The children were thirsty and tired so we stopped at a grocery store to get some treats. *"Give me some orange pop,"* says Kevin! *"I want pop, too,"* says Karen, Jane, Julie, Darwin, and David. *"What is that?"* asks the clerk? These folks had no idea what pop was! Finally, she realized we meant a soda! Culture shock! We were in for a new education. It was a new life, a new veterinary practice, a new jail ministry, new friends, and a new mission. More, IT WAS HOT—104°F HOT!

Renting a house in Eagle Pass was almost impossible. We finally rented one at 368 Pecos Street across from an empty lot. We moved the first of October and with permission from the city moved the trailer onto an empty lot next to the house and made it the veterinary clinic. My first call was a request to do a poodle trim. So, I did my first of many poodle trims and dog haircuts in Eagle Pass.

The children needed bicycles. We found a man uptown selling parts to bicycles. His place was like a junkyard, except instead of wrecked vehicles it was for old bicycles. I asked the man, *"How much for all these parts?"* He gave me a price, and we bought all the parts. Several pickup loads later, my boys and I started on the process of building bicycles. The boys and I made fourteen from that pile of parts. We sold some and used some. That summer was a precious time with the family. I helped the boys clean parts, and we put those bikes back together. We painted and fixed. On one bicycle, I welded a steering wheel in place of handlebars. We had run out of traditional handlebars by this point in the assembly of the bikes. This was my first experience with welding, but it was necessary to make these new bicycles. Well! Kevin was selected as the test pilot of this new bicycle. Kevin tried it out and started down a steep hill and the steering wheel came off! He crash landed, but did not get hurt. I think he told me to try again. This, of course, is one of the family stories at those annual reunions of today. They do not let me off lightly—they embellish the stories about my early welding skills.

We had family devotions daily and invited the neighbor children. Many came because they liked that bike project.

We met Arlene Fetter (a missionary) at this place. We met a number of other local missionaries such as Ruth Reffit and Enola, Betty, and Clair Gibson. We met Harland Cary, the President and lawn mower at Collegio Biblico. This college brought men and women from Mexico to study God's Word and prepare them for mission work in Mexico. I attended some classes there to help me learn Spanish. Joe Moreno, my next door neighbor, also helped with my Spanish. Another couple of missionary families that become close friends to our family included Mike and Evelyn Gary and Charles and Gloria Johnson.

I tried to integrate my newfound faith into every aspect of my life. This, however, created a conflict with the Texas Veterinary Medical Association as I opened my new practice in 1968. JoAnne and I purchased the receipt books for the new business. The name at the top read Eagle Pass Veterinary Clinic. On the bottom, I had *John* 1:12 printed:

> *"But as many as received Him, to them gave He power*
> *to become the sons of God, even to them that believe on*
> *His name."*

I was hoping to provide some exposure to the Gospel as clients came to my new practice. After about three months, I received an official letter and reprimand from the Texas Veterinary Medical Association telling me to get that *Bible* verse off the receipt. Someone in the Eagle Pass area was offended by that *Bible* verse and reported me to the officials. I never knew who it was, but God bless them and help them to see the real light! Even today, it is alarming to see the level of effort in which various entities strive to strip God out of every aspect of our public lives. These individuals want prayer out, the Ten Commandments off the wall, and the phrase *"Under God"* removed from the Pledge of Allegiance. Lord, help God's people to stand up and be counted!

Gil Heegard told me about Hope Mission in Eagle Pass, Texas.

Brother and Sister Hluchan were in charge. They gave beans and rice to poor folks who came to services at their small church. The Lord impressed on my *inner man* that I needed to find this mission and this Pastor Hluchan.

I thought this mission church was in Piedras Negras, the sister city across the Rio Grande River. One day I went to look for him. I drove to Mexico and parked by the market. Lord, help me find Hluchan, I prayed! The first man at the market that I talked to spoke English and said *"Brother Hluchan, I know him. He lives in Eagle Pass next to the mission. I will take you to him."* So, my new friend, Francisco Garcia, went with me and introduced me to Brother Hluchan.

Brother Hluchan and his wife lived very plainly. They got along with only the essentials, and from the start I knew he loved the Lord Jesus with all his heart. *"Brother Hluchan, I would like to have services in the jail in Eagle Pass, but I need an interpreter. Will you come and help me to reach the boys in jail with the gospel?"* He said he would be delighted to help, and so we started the next week and this relationship lasted about twelve years. I would preach in English, and Hluchan would interpret into Spanish. We would have an altar call and many responded. We gave each one a *New Testament* in Spanish or English, as needed. Inside each testament was a piece of paper with this message, "How to find Christ the Bible way."

This message was later sent to every home or post office box in Maverick County (the county surrounding Eagle Pass). Gospel tracts and this message in both Spanish and English were shipped from Dallas like a grocery store flyer. The people who were a part of Kings Way Bible Fellowship and Camino El Rey helped to stuff and seal all those letters. About 2,500 post office boxes were covered. The day of delivery, the garbage cans in the post office were

TO FIND SALVATION THE BIBLE WAY PLEASE STUDY THESE
CHAPTERS AND SPECIAL VERSES IN YOUR BIBLE. THEN
TALK TO GOD (PRAY) AND INVITE HIM INTO YOUR LIFE
AND HEART.

- John Chapter 1, note verse 12; John Chapter 3, note verse 16; and John Chapter 5, note verse 24
- Acts Chapter 3, note verse 19
- Romans Chapter 3, note verse 19 to 24; and Romans Chapter 12, note verse 1
- Galatians Chapter 3, note verse 24
- Ephesians Chapter 3, note verse 16
- 2nd Timothy Chapter 2, note verse 4
- 1st John Chapter 1, note verses 7 & 9; and 1st John Chapter 5, note verse 13
- Revelations Chapter 3, note verse 20
- Luke Chapter 23 and 24
- Isaiah Chapter 55, verse 7

Salvation, being saved, getting right with God requires a personal commitment or change. A person must say no to sin, ask for forgiveness, confess our sins to God and his son Christ Jesus and invite Christ Jesus into our hearts.

Then John 8:31–32 has the best direction for us to live this Christian life. Then said Jesus to those Jews which believe on him,
   "If ye continue in my Word, (study the Bible) then are ye my disciples indeed; and ye shall know the truth, and the truth shall make you free."

And then in verse 36,
   "If the son (Jesus) therefore shall make you free, ye shall be free indeed."

This homemade gospel tract was placed in each New Testament and Bible given away as part of my mission outreach. These were printed in English and Spanish.   Provided by Hans Peterson.

full of our letters. We did receive three inquiries in English and Camino El Rey received about six inquiries in Spanish. I know of one lady and her two children who were helped by this mail-out campaign and made commitments to Christ and also were baptized in water.

Pastor and Mrs. Hluchen became a part of our family. Besides the jail work, they often came for supper and had devotions with us. One day, Mrs. Hluchen brought her bedspread over for JoAnne to wash. It literally fell apart in the washer. JoAnne was very sorry about this—when she took it out of the machine, it was just in shreds. *"Oh, that's okay,"* said Sister Hluchen, *"it has not been washed for seventeen years!"*

One time Pastor Hluchen planted potatoes, and to protect them from insects he put mothballs around the plants. They always used a lot of mothballs for the used clothing that they gave away at the mission. When he dug up the potatoes and boiled them, they tasted and smelled like mothballs, so he had to throw them all away.

The mission board, the Pentecostal Church of God, built a home for Mr. and Mrs. Hluchen, which they lived in for about four years. Sister Hluchen's health was failing, so they were moved to Austin to a retirement home run by the church. That was in the 1982 timeframe. They have both since gone to be with Jesus. We were blessed as a family to have known both of them.

When Pastor Hluchen left, I continued the jail services alone. Over those years, I learned enough Spanish so I could read the *Bible* and preach in Spanish. Because of the veterinary work, I could also communicate with my clients in Spanish. The children also learned some Spanish (in varying degrees) and have found that in many places it is a blessing to them. The Spanish language has helped them in their work as well.

Hebrews 13:2 talks about showing hospitality to strangers.
Verse 5 says:

> *"Let your conversation be without covetousness; and be*
> *content with such things as ye have: for he hath said, I*
> *will never leave thee, nor forsake thee."*

JoAnne taught the above spiritual truth to our children, by the
choices she made and the example of the life she lives. She followed me willingly and worked beside me. We were a long way
from family or anything familiar. Our home became a stopping
place for missionaries from Mexico who had not seen running
water or ice cream for several years. They would stay with us for
a few hours, or a few days, on their way to and from deputation
and fund raising duties in the states. Jo could feed a crew on very
short notice. She demonstrated contentment despite the isola-
tion, as we trusted God together to lead us in the plan He had for
our lives. During this period of time, our 8th child, Stanley, was
born on May 7, 1971. *The only full Texan of the lot!*

Pastor Charles (Chuck) and Gloria Johnson lived in Eagle Pass
when we arrived, and we soon met them. They had four boys and
one girl in their family and were a big blessing to all of us. The
children liked to play together.

Chuck and Gloria were missionaries and were happy to have
us minister with them. Many Sunday mornings the boys, David,
Darwin, and Kevin, would go along with the Johnson's to minister to the Indians in the Kickapoo Village under the international
bridge in Eagle Pass. At the time, the Kickapoo Tribe lived in card-
board box homes supported with river cane rafters. They are citizens of Mexico, Canada, and the United States at birth. The

Johnson's would hold these services while Hluchan and myself were preaching at the jail.

On Sunday afternoons, Pastor Chuck, Brother Martinez, sometimes Brothers Juan Valenzuela, and Bob Manuel (with Teen Challenge) and I would go to the penitentiary in Piedras Negras, Coahuila Mexico. There were about 80 to 180 prisoners in this prison. A few were Anglos, but most were Hispanic and only spoke Spanish. In this jail setting, we were put right inside with the prisoners—no bars between them and us. The guards would walk above us on concrete catwalks with their guns over their shoulders and observe the inmates and visitors below.

Brother Chuck Johnson and Brother Juan Valenzuela, of course, spoke Spanish and preached the gospel. These men loved to have a service and usually from 20 to 100 men would come to the cafeteria to sit on the concrete benches or tables and listen. These men were supplied with *New Testaments* and some received *Bibles* to study during the week. After going to this jail for about a year, we had a baptismal service. I had the privilege of supplying the baptistery for that service, and Chuck Johnson talked the guards into letting us bring it into the jail that afternoon. About fifty men were baptized that day in a 50-gallon barrel! We had to add water after every three or four men because when they went under the water poured out over the top.

Bill Nelson, an Anglo American, was in jail for several years. I would visit with him after the service and slip him a few dollars to barter with the next week. Those men who were incarcerated had to earn their own keep by making trinkets. Birds, fish or other carvings were made from horns of cattle or from old fruit boxes and then sold to shop keepers in Piedras Negras. When shopping at the market in Mexico, I would recognize some of those wares made in the prison. Bill Nelson visited and stayed with us overnight when he was released from prison. He thanked us for the help, and we never saw him again.

From these experiences, I wrote the following song, back in the early 1970s, with the title *I Was In Sin's Prison:*

"I was in sin's prison, Oh so dark and cold.
Just a lost sheep wandering from God's eternal fold.
But the doors swung open, Jesus spoke to me, I have
signed your pardon, you may now go free.

CHORUS:
Yes, Jesus signed my pardon, this I surely know,
He took my place on Calvary, Now I won't have to go.
All my life I'll give to Him, He gave His for me.
When He signed my pardon there on Calvary.

My life is now worth living, since I have been set free.
I'm glad that He was willing to save a wretch like me.
Now, I have a mansion, not a prison wall.
Jesus signed my pardon, Oh yes He paid it all."

After living in town on 368 Pecos Street for several years, JoAnne and I moved the family and my practice out of town a little ways. The new place was located off of Eidson Road in Eagle Pass, Texas. Besides my veterinary practice, we started a small farming operation and later branched out into a feed and seed store business. We built our own home at this location and all the family got involved with the construction in one way or the other.

In 1974, we met the Rosalas family when they moved in next door to our home on Eidson Road. Their two sons were three and six years old. Danny was the oldest. About six months after they moved in, their youngest boy fell into the canal behind our place. I walked up the canal holding hands with Mr. Rosalas as we tried to find the body, but to no avail. The Fire Department located his little lifeless body about six hours later.

Danny became a friend and frequent playmate at our house. His parents split up, and Danny was left on his own much of the time. Danny came to *Bible* studies at our house some and was exposed to the King of Kings, Jesus Christ.

In 1986, Danny was in jail when I came to preach! He received a *New Testament* again and listened pretty well. Theft was the charge! Later, I counseled with Danny and a new girlfriend who was already pregnant. In about 1991, Danny called from San Antonio, Texas. *"Thanks for not giving up on me, Doc. I have a job, a nice family, and we are going to church every Sunday."* Lord, help Danny to remain faithful to You! Amen!

Another man I remember from our jail work was tall and young, but charged with murder. Brother Hluchen and myself ministered to him, Juan (not his real name) for six months. He was convicted of murder and sent to prison at Huntsville, Texas. About ten years later, Juan stopped me as I was shopping at the mall in Eagle Pass. *"Do you remember me?"* he said.

"No sir," was my response.

He said, *"Thanks for helping me at the jail. I am a Christian now and am married and have two children."* He gave me a 'bear hug' and thanked me again. JoAnne was along and said, *"Who was that?"*

Another man, Juan #2 (not his real name) was in jail in Eagle Pass for one year. From day one, he listened to the service and soon was helping each week. He also read and had Bible study with the other prisoners during the week. Brother Hluchen and I were very happy for Juan #2 when he was to be released from prison. Then, he called Brother Hluchen and told him his message was all-wrong, and that he would soon show us how to reach Mexico for Christ. He also informed me that he didn't believe all the things we were teaching, and that he was going to do it right.

Juan #2 was released. He went to Mexico and hitched a ride with a professional man to go south on Highway 57. The Mexican Paper, *The Zocalo*, carried the story on how their car was struck by a bus on that highway. It included a very graphic picture of the tragic scene of the accident. Juan #2's head was about four feet from the body. All of this occurred within a 24-hour period.

The two different responses to the Lord's message and the different paths they led to, for both Juan's from their prison experiences, is like the two criminals crucified on each side of Jesus. It is explained in *Luke* 23:39–43.

> *"And one of the malefactors which were hanged railed on him, saying, If thou be Christ, save yourself and us. But the other answering rebuked him, saying, Dost not thou fear God, seeing thou art in the same condemnation? And we indeed justly; for we receive the due reward of our deeds: but this man hath done nothing amiss. And he said unto Jesus, Lord, remember me when thou comest into thy kingdom. And Jesus said unto him, Verify I say unto thee, Today shalt thou be with me in paradise."*

Don't mess with God! I want that message to get to all my children, my grandchildren, my great-grand children, in-laws, and out-laws! Don't mess with God or the Scriptures! The message of the Word of God is for real. *John* 8:36 states:

"If the Son therefore shall make you free, ye shall be free indeed."

Don't let that old world nature win—yield to King Jesus!

My parents visited us in Eagle Pass several times. I recall one of those visits was for Thanksgiving. Right before we were to sit down for our Thanksgiving meal, the phone rang. It was for my dad. He was informed that his son, my brother Curtis, had been wounded in Vietnam. All they could tell Dad for sure was that his head was not injured. Curtis later recovered from his injuries, but the soldier in front of him that stepped on the landmine was killed.

On another visit from my folks, at Christmas time, we received a wonderful gift that has become a family keepsake. My mom had packed a large box with a very heavy gift for their bus trip from Minnesota to Texas. She did not tell Dad what was in the box, but he was required to move this uncomfortable load multiple times prior to making it to our house in Texas. I gathered he was not thrilled to transport such a burden on his holiday vacation. When we opened it at Christmas, it turned out to be Dad's large brass bell off a train that he had picked up at one of his auction sales. He seemed shocked to see that my mom had given his bell away for Christmas! My mom was a collector of all types of bells; it was a hobby for her. Thanks, Dad; we used that bell to call the boys out of the hog barn for many years! Yes, a hog barn, and about one acre of concrete poured with a small cement mixer on the Eidson Road place. Dad and I spoke of spiritual things at times during those visits, and he said he was trusting only Christ for his salvation. My Dad went to be with the Lord at age 87 during the time we lived in Eagle Pass.

In 1991, the old Eagle Pass jail was closed and the new jail was very difficult for me. It seemed to me that it was not safe and that prisoners could overpower the guards and escape! So, after twenty-two years of jail service, I decided new blood, new men should take over this work. The Lord released me and gave me peace. Through this ministry, I was afforded the privilege to distribute an estimated 30 thousand *New Testaments* and 3 thousand complete *Bibles* to Mexico and South America to these inmates as they returned home after their prison terms.

I want to give a special thanks to Brother and Sister Hluchan, Chuck and Gloria Johnson, Mike and Evelyn Gary, Al and Fran Johnson, Bernice Oser, and Bill and Virginia Perry for their help in the ministry and support of my family while we lived in Eagle Pass, Texas.

I continued to practice veterinary medicine and started and operated a feed business in Eagle Pass over the years. This was an important addition to my practice, and I enjoyed being able to teach many of my clients about the nutritional needs of their animals. The veterinary practice in Eagle Pass, Texas was different than the one in Minnesota. Down on the border there were two large feedlots with 20,000 plus head of cattle each and these presented some new challenges to me as a vet from up north. I had the privilege to work with both of these feedlots for about five years and then off and on after that.

Cesarean sections to remove a newborn calf from a mother cow are always a challenge. In Minnesota, I had done several cesareans in a pole barn when it was 15 to 20 degrees below zero. The heat from the cow kept you warm enough to work. In Eagle Pass, I recall one night I did a cesarean using two flashlights as my only illumination. The cow and newborn calf lived, and the lady who helped said it was more exciting than Mash on TV!

A large part of the volume of the veterinary practice in Eagle Pass consisted of treating small animals in my clinic. While on occasions I worked on animals such as parrots, turtles and rabbits, mainly I worked on dogs and cats. Shown below is a photo of me working on a large Doberman pincher in my office.

I am giving an eye exam to my own dog, Hilda. Hilda was a Doberman Pincher and served as my blood donor when I needed to give transfusions to other dogs during treatment.
Photo courtesy of Peterson Portrait Design.

I also experienced several rare events in my practice in south Texas. One of these occurred in 1969. During that year, equine encephalomyelitis of the Venezuela type (called VEE) entered Texas from Mexico at Maverick and Dimmit Counties. VEE and the other sleeping sickness-type diseases are caused by a virus. This virus is transmitted by mosquitoes. About seventeen horses died from the disease in Maverick County in two months, that I knew about. Other vets I and tried to treat this disease to no avail. It spread very rapidly and was fatal in less than 72 hours. The Venezuela type was deadly, and the horses went crazy! Some would start running; they would run wild, straight through fences and then fall down, thrashing and beating their heads on the ground. One horse that I will never forget fell into an irrigation ditch made of concrete. It was about five feet across at the bottom with slanted sides. The horse's head would touch the water and he would pick it up and slam his head against the concrete. We could do nothing! He killed himself as he pounded his head on the concrete.

Another rare event occurred in 1979. From March to November, we had a rabies epidemic in Maverick County. I wrote an article about this problem that was published in *Modern Vet Practice*, May 1980. The article, in its entirety, is provided here:

Rabies Protection: A Better Approach by Hans Peterson, DVM

In Maverick County, Texas from March 19 to November 20, 1979, 106 animal heads were examined by the Texas Department of Health Laboratories for rabies. Of these, 20 dog heads were fluorescent antibody test-positive. At least 72 persons considered exposed to these 20 dogs received the full 23-dose series of duck embryo vaccine (DEV), and some received rabies immune globulin as well. Two young persons in this county died of rabies in 1979, and I have asked myself why, many, many times.

*All animals are subject to rabies, but it occurs most fre-
quently in the wolf, cat, skunk and dog, and is chiefly prop-
agated by dogs. The virus has a special affinity for the
nervous tissue and is found in secretions, particularly saliva.
In man there are usually 3 stages of the disease. The prelim-
inary stage is characterized by marked restlessness, appre-
hension and obvious ill health. In the second ("furious")
stage the patient is hyperactive and has spasms of the muscles of swallowing and respiration. The third stage is
marked by drooling saliva due to the poor control of throat,
tongue and laryngeal muscles.*

*On the morning of March 14, 1979, Mr. John Doe (a client
of mine, will refer to him as Mr. John Doe) of Maverick
County brought his dog to my clinic with the complaint that
the animal was not acting properly. The dog, a large male
Shepherd-cross about 2 years old, had been ill for about 2
days, and his coat was dirty with clay.*

*"Seems to have something stuck in his throat, Doc," John
said. One look at the dog told me the tongue was paralyzed,
and although I had not seen a rabid dog in my 19 years of
practice, this one was an obvious suspect. After I explained
that the disease was very likely rabies and that the dog was
unvaccinated, John agreed I should destroy the animal and
send the head for rabies diagnosis. For euthanasia I general-
ly use the cephalic vein, but due to the close proximity to the
head I made the injection in the hind leg. As the dog went
to sleep it kicked, and the needle punctured my thumb.*

Dr. Hans Peterson (left) vaccinates a young dog.
Photo courtesy of Core Publishing & Consulting, Inc.

Oh well, I thought, maybe it doesn't have rabies after all. Rabies analysis 4 days later, however, confirmed the animal positive for rabies. The Department of Health officials originally told me I was not exposed, but after I asked if it were possible for rabies virus and saliva to be on the hind leg of the dog when it was presented at the clinic, I was told, yes, it was possible. If the needle picked up virus going through the hair and saliva, could the virus already be in the nerves of my hand, and if so, what happens next? The official replied, "You get rabies!"

On March 20, the Department of Health began giving me

the 23 doses of duck embryo vaccine (DEV) and rabies
immune globulin. Reactions from the injections were 2 to 4
inches in diameter, red, and very itchy. With this, I began a
summer I will not easily forget.

Date Animal Presented	Date Rabies Confirmed	No. of Persons Exposed	Vaccine Begun	Comments
	Chronological Listing of Rabies Cases, March 19, 1979 through November 24, 1979, Eagle Pass, Texas			
3/14/79	3/19/79	1	6 days	Lingual paralysis, sick about 3 days, not vaccinated
4/18/79	4/20/79	17	8 days	Presented dead, signs had been consistent with furious rabies
4/20/79	4/26/79	31	8 days	
4/21/79	4/26/79	1	5 days	Died at dog pound, tongue protruding from mouth
4/21/79	4/26/79	0		Died at dog pound, lingual paralysis
4/21/79	4/26/79	0		Died comatose, lingual paralysis
4/23/79	4/27/79	0		Dumb rabies signs
4/26/79	5/1/79	0		Picked up dead on street
5/3/79	5/8/79	0		This dog pursued another until she had bitten her
5/14/79	5/17/79	0		
5/25/79	5/31/79	0		Lingual paralysis, slobbering
5/31/79	6/5/79	9	6 days	One child sickened and died after 21 doses of DEV
5/31/79	6/5/79	2	6 days	Vaccinated on 5-12-79, street virus identified
6/27/79	6/31/79	1	4 days	
6/30/79	7/3/79	0		
7/20/79	7/25/79	0		
7/23/79	7/28/79	0		Vaccinated 7-13-79
8/9/79	8/9/79	4	2 days	Vaccinated 7-24-79, street virus identified
9/7/79	9/11/79	0		Stray picked up dead on street
9/18/79	9/20/79	9	4 days	Owner had picked up this stray 30 days earlier at city limits. Not vaccinated. Typical furious rabies.
11/20/79	11/24/79	0		Fox came in yard within city limits

Of the 9 persons bitten by these dogs later proven to be
rabid, 3 did not start treatment until 5–8 days after expo-
sure. Because exposure was usually 2–3 days prior to suspi-
cion of rabies, shipping and testing resulted in further delay.

Photo courtesy of Courtesy of Core Publishing & Consulting, Inc.

Yes, the vaccine protected me from getting rabies — or did it?
Perhaps I was not exposed, and the injections only protected
me from further exposure. One of the 2 local (Eagle Pass)
children that died from rabies had received 21 doses of DEV
before symptoms of rabies were seen. She began the series of
vaccine 6 days after the bite wound was inflicted.

Deaths have been reported in several cases in which the
course of DEV treatment was not started immediately or

was not completed. How many individuals begin anti-rabies treatment before 5 days have elapsed after being bitten by a non-vaccinated dog?

HOW BETTER TO PROTECT THE PUBLIC?

What needs to be done to better protect the public from rabies? There are 2 ways in which more complete protection can be provided. The first concerns the use of human diploid cell vaccine (HDCV).

During outbreaks of rabies in Iran, the brain tissue vaccine in common use failed to protect individuals severely exposed, many of whom developed the disease and died shortly after exposure. This vaccine also triggered severe reactions, resulting in partial or total post-vaccination paralysis and even death, while DEV elicited poor antigenic responses. Researchers evaluating the use of HDCV in these outbreaks concluded: "A major breakthrough has been achieved in the post-exposure treatment of humans exposed to rabies." Six or fewer injections were highly immunogenic, and the vaccine caused virtually no side effects.

The Center for Disease Control in Atlanta has found HDCV to be very efficacious and safe. Reactions have not been as frequent or severe as with DEV and 5 or 6 injections produce an antibody response about 10 times that achieved with DEV. All of 188 persons given ≥3 doses of HDCV developed titers ≥1:16, whereas titers developed in only 80–92% of persons given 2–23 doses of DEV. From these data and local experience it appears that one of every 10 persons given the

*present DEV series, and who are actually incubating the
virus, will not receive protection and will die from rabies.*

*A resolution passed by the Texas VMA at its 1979 meeting
urged Wyeth Laboratories and the human biologics licens-
ing division of USPHS "to proceed together in the utmost
urgency, to produce and distribute for use in humans at the
earliest possible date, the human diploid cell line rabies vaccine."*

*The second part of the solution is to begin anti-rabies treat-
ment immediately when a person has an actual bite wound
from an unvaccinated animal. It should not start after the
diagnosis is made as experience last summer shows that this
delays the beginning of treatment for up to 8 days (see
chart).*

Conclusion
*To help solve the human rabies problem in endemic areas
will require: (1) starting vaccination immediately for persons bitten by unknown animals or those known to be
unvaccinated; and (2) use of the human diploid cell line
vaccine to stimulate rapid immunity to the disease.*

References:
• *Morbidly Mortality Weekly Rept 25(51), Dec 31, 1976.*
• *J Amer Med Assn 236(24): Dec, 1976.*
• *Baker, E.F.: Personal Communication, April 9–11, 1979.*
• *Texas Vet Med J 41:12, 1979.*

My veterinary career allowed me to spend an extra amount of time actively involved in the daily lives of my family; most professional careers of today would not afford this blessing. In addition to my veterinary practice, I started a hog farming operation to keep my boys busy. The boys like to tell the story that we could not have any horses because I insisted that everything on the farm pay its own way. Thus, we had cows that the boys milked by hand, hogs that we sold to market, chickens that we made Mom clean to help feed the family, dogs that were blood donors for my clinic and cats that.... What do cats do? Well, they killed rats that would rob the hog feed, and charm rattlesnakes. And charm rattlesnakes? Yes, I know this for a fact.

One morning, I stepped out the back door of my clinic on to the first step. This opened up to a covered carport patio for my veterinary pickup. I had never seen or heard a real rattlesnake in my life, but by the sound I heard that morning, I knew I was only a few feet away from one! I jumped and went airborne from nearly the back tire of the truck to near the front tire and tried to land on a small worktable over to the side. The table tipped and I ended up in front of the truck with scratches as I fell to the ground. I quickly looked under the truck to see why the snake had not tried to strike me. I was shocked to see one of my Siamese cats sitting quietly only a foot or so from the 4-foot long rattlesnake that was coiled up ready to strike. Since my clinic was only about 75 feet from our house, I was terrified that one of my eight children would come walking by any minute. I jumped in the truck and maneuvered it to run over the snake and eliminate the immediate danger to the family. Thus, my Siamese cats were indeed a solid investment. Over the years in Eagle Pass, I treated a number of rattlesnake bite wounds on animals. Those animals that had been bitten in the chest close to their hearts would die. All the other bitten animals, once treated, would survive.

The boys did not get their horse wish, however, they did have a good friend (Harland Cary) down the road with horses and mules and our children were occasionally allowed to go ride. This friend, Harland Carry, got me in *hot water* with Jo once, though. He talked me into de-scenting baby skunks that he wanted to keep as pets. The first batch of operations went fine. However, when I got sprayed during one of the subsequent operations, Jo informed me that my operating days on skunks were over. Thanks, but no thanks, Harland!

After the six oldest children had gone on to college and started to get married, JoAnne, Sandra, Stanley and I moved back into town. We moved to 800 Yota and Airport Road across from a large mall in Eagle Pass. We built a large two-story complex with an apartment on the second level. My veterinary clinic, tire store and feed-and-seed store operations were on the lower level. We also built an eight-unit apartment complex behind these businesses. Later, I opened a second store in Piedras Negras, Mexico.

In the later years in Eagle Pass, after my jail ministry was winding down and most of our children had graduated from high school, JoAnne, the remaining children at home and I worshipped with Bill and Virginia Perry at Quemado, Texas in their small country church. Sister Izzy Fremer, 'Virginia's sister, and Sister Williams were always there. Bill Perry, or Billy as we sometimes called him, would exchange our share of jokes and jabs. My favorite joke is about St. Peter's Gate:

> *At St. Peter's Gate, Peter asked, "What have you done to deserve to go to heaven?*

There are 100 points required! You tell me what you
have done in your life and I will give the points."

"Okay. I went to Sunday school and had perfect attendance for 8 years and studied my lesson each week."

"That's great, Hans. That gives you 2 points. What
else?"

"Well, I have gone to jails and preached the gospel and
gave New Testaments to prisoners for about thirty
years."

"That's great, Hans, and your get 2 more points. What
else?"

'Well, I have given some folks in need some money, gas
for their cars and helped fix their cars over the years."

'Oh, that's great, Hans. I give you 2 more points. What
else?"

"My, if that is all the points, by your rules, it is going to
take the grace of God to get into heaven!"

"Bingo," said St. Peter. "By God's grace you can come
in."

Virginia Perry was the Pastor of the Assembly of God church
in Quemado. JoAnne and I really looked forward to our time of
worship in this small country church. We sang the old time gospel

hymns. A song that became dear to my heart is *A Crown of Thorns* by Ira Stanphill:

> *There was no crown for Him of silver or of gold.*
> *There was no diadem for Him to hold.*
> *But blood adorned His brow and proud its stain He*
> *bore,*
> *And sinners gave to Him the crown He wore.*

> Chorus:
> *A rugged cross, became His throne.*
> *His kingdom was in hearts alone.*
> *He wrote His love in crimson red,*
> *And wore the thorns upon His Head.*

> *He did not reign upon a throne of ivory,*
> *But died upon the cross of Calvary.*
> *For sinners there He counted all He owned but loss.*
> *And He surveyed His Kingdom from a cross.*

> *No purple robe He wore His bleeding wounds to hide,*
> *But stripes upon His back He wore with pride.*
> *And from the wounds there flowed a crimson, cleansing*
> *stream,*
> *That was a cover for the soul unclean.*

I recall one special Sunday service, a stranger (to me at least) came to the service. He had lost his mother recently and wanted Virginia to have a memorial service for her. This lady had been dead and buried about six months earlier, and this man had been unable to attend the funeral. We sang some hymns, Virginia preached about death and resurrection. The man told a few memories of his mother, and we all remembered her family in prayer. I remember it being a precious service that touched my *inner man.*

This memorial service was similar to the Lord's Supper, a communion service as described in *I Corinthians,* 11:23–26:

> *"For I have received of the Lord that which also I deliv-*
> *ered unto you, That the Lord Jesus the same night in*
> *which he was betrayed took bread. And when he had*
> *given thanks, he brake it, and said, Take, eat: this is my*
> *body which is broken for you: this do in remembrance*
> *of me. After the same manner also he took the cup,*
> *when he had supped, saying, This cup is the New*
> *Testament in my blood: this do ye, as oft as ye drink it,*
> *in remembrance of me. For as often as ye eat this bread,*
> *and drink this cup, ye do show the Lord's death till he*
> *come."*

It is a memorial service and when done in this manner: in remembrance of Christ, in remembrance of the whipping He endured, in remembrance of His crown of thorns, in remembrance of the cruel nails through His hands and feet, in remembrance of the words He spoke. In *Luke* 23:34 we find:

> *"Then said Jesus, Father, forgive them; for they know*
> *not what they do. And they parted his raiment, and cast*
> *lots."*

Luke 22:18, reminds us of Jesus' words:

"For I say unto you, I will not drink of the fruit of the vine, until the kingdom of God shall come."

This communion service is a real blessing to me and if you read the old, old story again, it will be to you also. *In remembrance of Christ! Glory to God!*

JoAnne and I were also re-examining our lives at this point in time. What was God's next step for us? JoAnne and I decided to purchase the Kaufman Feed Store from A. O. Freeman on February 1, 1993. This feed store was located in Kaufman Texas. Kaufman is a small town, southeast and not far from Dallas, Texas. My oldest son, David, who had spent the prior twelve years as owner of a photography business in Lewisville, Texas, was ready for a new challenge in life. He started off as business manager of this new operation for JoAnne and myself.

As we continued to seek for the leading of God's Spirit, both Jo and I knew one thing about God without any doubts. **The life lesson we learned from these years on the mission field and raising our family was:** *"God's Word and Plans withstand the trials of life and the test of time."*

CHAPTER ELEVEN

North Texas Current Years

In January of 1994, JoAnne and I sold out our business interests and property in Eagle Pass and moved north to Kaufman, Texas. JoAnne and I were moving to be closer to many of our children and ever-growing number of grandchildren who were predominately living near the Dallas metroplex. We joined David and Carolyn in the operation of our feed store, the Kaufman Feed Store. I also opened a veterinarian office.

When JoAnne and I first arrived up in Kaufman, my mom was still alive. My mom was 94 years young when she wrote this letter to me in 1998:

"Dear Hans,

1998 minus 1933 makes you 65 years. That's a long time to remember whom your dad talked about. But one was Pastor Lund—he must have been his mentor besides the one who was auctioneer at that time and his school-

teacher friends and the man he farmed with when he was 16.

All my life I've had so many relatives on my mind. I can't remember my own children's doings when you all grew up and wanted to get married. Then I was out of raising and controlling you. I remember some things I did wrong. But nothing I did right. Old age gives a person time to think and wonder.

Soon your birthday—you have always done the right things in my eyes—but it seems my children are not close to each other—am I just imagining it?

We are having wonderful winter—no cold fingers and cold feet.

Had valentine from Kevin and Deena. I bet they are happy about a baby.

Robert has a lot of pain in his heel. Wonder why.

The sheets & pillowcases are beautiful and all other things you have given me I thank you. Some of our folks are sick. Some are in hospital—so guess that's life and young or old get sore spots.

I proud of all the good things you do for your family and for all of the other folks who need help & comfort.

With love, Mom."

JoAnne and I would try to visit mom during the summers and stay in regular phone contact during the remainder of the year. Mom was a miracle of joy and love. She was always looking for articles about the family or maybe a picture she could share with us. I recall from one of those evening phone calls mom told me she had attended Mrs. Gehard Swenson' funeral the week before. Gehard and Cora Swenson were good friends of both JoAnne's and my parents over the years. I recall from my youth that Gehard was the *clown* of the local township when he was a young man. He turned out to be a really good farmer as well as a person always willing to help other neighbors. If you needed help, Gehard would be there to fix a barn door, castrate calves, or shingle a roof.

The thought of Gehard shingling a roof brings up a classic reunion tale. One time Gehard came to repair the roof of Art Jackson's barn (JoAnne's father) and it was very steep. Art told him to be careful and put this rope on so if he fell he could catch himself. *"Okay,"* said Gehard, and he climbed up to the top of the roof. When he came in sight after climbing up, Art saw he had the rope around his neck! Art did not know if he fell, should he pull on the rope or let it go? Later that same day, he stood on his head on top of the barn!

My customers in veterinary medicine have given me many interesting stories over the years as well. For example, on one cold winter day, a customer Carol from a farm to market road in Kaufman brought Hitler in to see me. Hitler was a male dachshund about two years old and weighed around fifteen pounds. She placed the dog on the exam table, and he had first degree burn marks on both back legs.

In trying to find out what caused these big sores, I said, *"Maybe he was bitten by another dog."* Carol said, *"Oh no, the dog is in a cage by himself."* I continued, *"Well, maybe he has been chewing himself and causing the damage?"*

She replied, *"No doctor, this dog doesn't have fleas; we use flea prevention once a month."*

So I asked, *"Have you fed Hitler any hot grease or fat after cooking?"*

"No way!" was the answer.

Then I looked at Carol and said, *"You tell me how the dog got burned."*

She hit the table with her hand, and said, *"I know! We had a light bulb burning in his dog house, and last week when we got up one morning, the little dog house was burned to the ground."*

I said, *"That could be the cause all right."* Hitler was treated with antibiotics and Hexicaine spray. Then I said, *"I bet he'll be fine now."*

Recently, there was a small brown and white pigmy goat trying to deliver a kid. The little nostrils were opening and shutting, telling me he was alive. With some strong yet gentle force, the mama pushed and delivered a live male baby goat. It is such a miracle; it thrills me even after 45 years of practicing veterinary medicine.

After David and I had been in business together for a number of years, JoAnne and I decided to sell the feed store portion of our interests out to David and his wife, Carolyn. David and Carolyn are now operating the feed store in Kaufman.

Upon initially arriving in Kaufman, JoAnne and I had built an apartment over the business. Once we sold out control of the business, JoAnne and I relocated to our current home in Terrell, Texas in 2001. David and I worked out an arrangement so that I could continue to operate a veterinary clinic from this facility. Terrell is reasonably close to Kaufman, so in addition to commuting to my vet practice, JoAnne and I continue to worship at Oak

Hill Church in Kaufman. We had attended this church for a number of years while living in Kaufman.

It was determined in the middle of 2002 that I needed prostate surgery. However, after various tests were conducted, it was determined by a heart specialist that my heart needed attention first. I had experienced no problems, and it was a blessing that we learned of the condition of my heart. Five by-pass surgery was done on July 18. The doctor noted that there was some scar tissue on my heart from many years before. A crisis on the day after surgery required that I return to ICU. It was a scare for all of us at the hospital. What a blessing to have family and church friends praying. JoAnne has been so good to care for me and was able to get me back to work in a few weeks. Suffice it to say, when the cloud gets dark, there may not be time to call on God or to straighten out things left undone.

My advice, a life lesson I have learned, is: *"Be ready to meet King Jesus at any moment."* Thanks, God, for delaying that surgery for thirty-seven years.

I am still practicing veterinary medicine at the age of seventy-one. Why? I still enjoy this career choice I made as a little boy back on the farm in Minnesota. Like one of my sons said, *"It is now like a hobby to him, but he just happens to be one of the few that gets paid to do his hobby."* I am still interacting with the customers that I enjoy. Although, at this point in my career, I have no problem sending certain vet work down the road, if it is something I prefer not to handle anymore.

My family has experienced three losses over this past year. My daughter, Sandra, and her family lost an infant child, Brooke Tyler Dargel, in July 2003. My youngest brother, Dr. Curtis Peterson, went home to be with the Lord in February 2004. And, my mother, Lavilla Peterson, followed in March 2004. Brooke was one month old at the time of her passing, while my mother was over 100 years old.

Curtis was fifty-eight years old at the time of his death on February 23, 2004. Both Curtis and his wife, Marlys, have been a real blessing to JoAnne, my family, and me over the years. Six of us were able to make the trip to Alabama for Curtis's funeral. None that attended this funeral could escape seeing the tremendous impact that Curtis had on the lives he touched through his teaching, guiding adults to complete their GEDs, or ministering in his local church on what God can do. The Pastor, Dick Stark, shared during the funeral that Curtis was a man that was always about finishing projects that needed to be done. One of the last things he made sure his family completed was the dedication of his only grandson, Hampton, to the Lord in church. The dedication occurred the day prior to his death.

My oldest brother, Robert, and his wife, Eunice, and my younger brother, Ralph, and his wife, Jeanette, are living in Glenwood, Minnesota. My sister, Lila, and her husband, Tom, are living in Cottage Grove, Oregon. We all had an opportunity to visit with each other at my mom's funeral in Minnesota. Robert is currently undergoing treatment for prostate cancer, but still works some on a turkey farm. Like me, Ralph has recently undergone heart surgery to remove blockage. Although he is currently retired and completed a beautiful home overlooking Lake Minnewaska in Glenwood, on occasions he still serves to fill vacancies to help Lutheran churches out during periods of being without a full-time pastor on staff. Unlike the boys, Lila has not had to spend her time with the medical doctors—other than with her husband, Doctor Tom!

Lila took care of Mom for the past several years until Mom's death. Prior to this period, my sister-in-law, Eunice, and her daughter, Marilyn, and my other sister-in-law, Jeanette, all helped to care for Mom. I'm sure many others from the family contributed in ways that improved Mom's quality of life in her latter years, and I am grateful to each of these individuals.

At this point in my life, I am very grateful for what God has done for my family. As I have described, I was nothing on my own. God, through His master plan, created an instrument that He was able to use for His service. The foundational building blocks God used to transform my heart started with the seeds that my dad and mom planted as a young boy. My parents are gone today, but the lessons remain and impact me even now.

As I was finishing up this manuscript, our second son, Darwin, without any prior indication, experienced a stroke in the general region of the brain of the optic nerve. The stroke resulted in an immediate fifty percent loss of his peripheral eyesight. The long-term prognosis for what level of recovery Darwin is able to achieve is still unknown at this early stage following this event. Various medical options are being considered including surgery. As Darwin and his wife Nelda prepare to face this uncertain challenge ahead together, as a family we rely upon the expertise of the doctors entrusted with Darwin's care coupled with our prayers and trust in Our Lord. Adversity can strike a family at any point in time. I cannot imagine facing family crisis events, such as that of my son, without a personal relationship with Jesus Christ upon which I can lean.

CHAPTER TWELVE

My Family and Society Today

A ll eight children, my mom, JoAnne, and I are shown in this family photograph.

Hans and JoAnne Peterson and Family. Shown are three generations of my family at Hans' mother's 99th birthday celebration in 2002 in the basement of Barsness Lutheran Church. Darwin, Jane, Julie, Karen, Stan, Sandra, JoAnne, Lavilla, Hans, David, and Kevin.

Photo courtesy of Peterson Portrait Design.

This photograph was taken in May 2003 at a large birthday celebration for my mother when she turned 99. In addition to our eight children, some of the daughters-in-law, grandchildren, and great-grandchildren attended this historic Peterson event! It was fun to see so many relatives.

Our eight children are listed below by age. A more detailed description of their respective families is included following the list.

- ~ David Keith, born on July 20, 1954.
- ~ Darwin Lyle, born on July 26, 1955.
- ~ Kevin Dale, born on April 7, 1957.
- ~ Julie Anne, born on July 24, 1958.
- ~ Jane Lynn, born on February 15, 1960.
- ~ Karen Renae, born on November 2, 1961.
- ~ Sandra Jean, born on July 2, 1968.
- ~ Stanley John, born on May 7, 1971.

David graduated from Eagle Pass High school in 1972. He went to Angelo State University where he majored in pre-med. In 1974, he transferred to Texas Women's University and changed his major to nursing. In 1974, David met Carolyn Sue Murray, daughter of Paul and Phylis Murray. David and Carolyn were united in marriage January 4, 1975. David entered the photography industry in 1976, after the birth of their first child. He continued in photography until December 1972, when he and his wife, Carolyn, became partners in a feed business in Kaufman, Texas with JoAnne and I. David and Carolyn have recently acquired this feed store on their own and branched out to include saddle repair work and a photography studio. David received his certification from the Professional Photographers of America (PPA) in 1989 and his Masters of Photography from the PPA in 1996. Carolyn graduated from MacArthur High School in Irving, Texas in 1970. She attended Dallas Bible College from 1970–1971. She received her Executive Secretary Diploma from Draughon's Business College of Dallas, Texas in 1972. David and Carolyn have three children and five grandchildren as summarized below:

~ Jennifer Lynn, born January 25, 1976, married Gregory Davidson on July 16, 1993. They have three children:

   ◦ Kristen Lauren, born December 17, 1993.

   ◦ Jonathan Ray, born September 29, 2000.

   ◦ Allysen Grace, born October 11, 2002.

~ David Daniel, born February 17, 1978, is single and is currently a veterinary student at Texas A&M University.

The David and Carolyn Peterson Family (2003). Robert and Janel (Peterson) Hicks and their two children, James and Adam. David and Carolyn (Murray) Peterson and their son, David Daniel. Greg and Jennifer (Peterson) Davidson and their three children, Kristen, Jonathan, and Allysen.

Photo courtesy of Peterson Portrait Design.

~ Janell Ruth, born July 10, 1979, married Robert James Hicks on February 20, 1999. They have two children:
  o James Paul, born October 2, 1999.
  o Adam Keith, born April 24, 2003.

Darwin graduated from Eagle Pass High School in 1974 and went to Southwest Texas Junior College and then transferred to Southwest Texas State University to complete his undergraduate degree in Criminal Justice. He married Nelda Gonzalez, daughter of Lou and Gloria Gonzalez, on May 17, 1980. Nelda graduated from Texas Tech University with a Bachelor of Arts degree in

The Darwin and Nelda (Gonzalez) Peterson Family (2000):
Darwin, Joshua, Jordan, Nelda, and Jared.

Photo courtesy of Darwin and Nelda Peterson and Peterson Portrait Design.

Audiology in 1980. She completed a Master degree in Diagnostic-Special Education from Southwest Texas State University in 2001. Darwin has worked for U.S. Immigration (now known as the Department of Homeland Security) for twenty-five years. He is a deportation officer working in San Antonio, Texas. Darwin and Nelda have three children.

~ Jordan Alejandro is single and recently returned from a tour of duty in Afganistan with the U.S. Army.

~ Joshua Aaron is currently a freshman at Texas Tech University, majoring in architecture.

~ Jared Adam is currently in the 10th grade.

The Kevin and Deena (Ketola) Peterson Family (1998): Deena, Tita, and Kevin.

Photo courtesy of Kevin and Deena Peterson
and Peterson Portrait Design.

Kevin graduated from Eagle Pass High School in 1976 and attended Texas A&M University. He received an undergraduate degree in Electrical Engineering in 1980. He later went back to night school and obtained a masters degree in Business Administration from Amber University in 1996. He married Deena Ketola, daughter of V. K. and Tita (Graillet) Ketola, on December 12, 1980. They surprised the family seventeen years later when their only child, a daughter named Tita Graillet Ketola Peterson, was born. She is currently six years old. Prior to Deena's father passing away, he nicknamed his granddaughter Pikku Tita which stands for Little Tita in Finnish, V. K.'s nationality.

Julie graduated from Eagle Pass High School in 1976 and went to Brazil as an exchange student with Rotary Club International her first year after graduation. She believes in life-long learning and has spent most of her life in the classroom. She received a B.A. in Humanities, with concentrations in English and Linguistics, from The University of Texas at Austin in 1980; a Graduate Bible Certificate from Dallas Bible College in 1982; and a M.A. in English in 1989, along with Secondary Teacher Certification in 1991, from the University of North Texas. Since 1995 she has also completed over sixty hours of coursework towards an Ed.D. in Curriculum and Instruction from the University of Houston. Her other experiences in the classroom include teaching several years of Bible classes as a missionary in Brazil; one year as a third grade teacher in Brazil; twelve years as an English-as-a-Second-Language secondary teacher in Baytown, TX; and one year as a high school reading teacher in West Palm Beach, FL. She married her husband David Blaylock, son of Charles Blaylock and Elaine Lisciandro, on December 21, 1980. David graduated from Dallas Bible College with a B.S. in

Psychology and Bible in 1983. He is currently a director of a substance abuse clinic in West Palm Beach. David and Julie have two children:

~ Brandon Dean was born on August 27, 1982, and is currently a senior at Louisiana State University in Baton Rouge, LA, majoring in Music Education.

~ Candice Lee was born on April 3, 1984, and is currently a sophomore at Midwestern State University in Wichita Falls, TX, studying to become a Biology teacher.

The David and Julie Blaylock Family: Brandon, Julie, David, and Candice and their two white German Shepard dogs.

Photo courtesy of Hans Peterson and Peterson Portrait Design.

After graduation from Eagle Pass High School in 1978, Jane attended the University of Texas at Austin and completed nursing school at the University of Texas Health Science Center in San

Antonio with a BSN degree in 1982. *True to her independent nature, Jane would become the only Peterson daughter not to choose a husband named David.* She and Michael Brode Leach, son of Willis B. and DeElva Leach, married on March 10, 1984, shortly before he graduated from UTHSC Dental School. Jane graduated with a Masters of Science in Nursing in 2004. She and Mike live in Wichita Falls, Texas and have four children:

~ Darla De was born on September 20, 1984, and is a student at Oklahoma State University majoring in landscape architecture.

~ (Michael) Brady was born on February 27, 1987. He is seventeen and in the 12th grade.

The Dr. Mike and Jane Leach Family (2003): Mike, Ana, Jane, John, Brady, and Darla.

Photo courtesy of Mike and Jane Leach.

∼ John Brode was born on May 12, 1992. He is twelve and
   in the 7th grade.

∼ Ana Jo was born on September 22, 1996. She is seven and
   in the 2nd grade.

Karen graduated from Eagle Pass High School in 1980 and
from Texas A&M University in 1983 with a degree in International
Marketing. She married David Harold Briles, Jr., son of Harold

The David and Karen Briles Family (2004). Deric,
David, Travis, and Karen.

Photo courtesy of David and Karen Briles.

and Edith (Bowman) Briles on May 25, 1985. David graduated with an undergraduate degree in business from the University of North Carolina, located in Chapel Hill North Carolina, in 1983. Karen operates a business doing Spanish interpreting and training. They live in Asheboro, North Carolina with their two boys:

~ Deric James was born on September 19, 1986. He is seventeen and in the 11th grade.

~ Travis Lee was born on April 9, 1989. He is fifteen and a freshman in high school.

Sandra graduated from Lewisville High School in 1986. During her senior year, she lived with David and Carolyn. She attended the University of North Texas and in 1990 received an undergraduate degree in elementary education. She went on to get a masters degree in 1993 in elementary education. She married David Alan Dargel, son of Duane and Betty Dargel, on June 8, 1991. David graduated with a Bachelor of Science degree from the Northern Illinois University in 1985. David and Sandra have four children still living, and a child who has gone to be with the Lord nearly a year ago:

~ Breanna Jo, born on April 6, 1993. She is eleven and in the 5th grade.

~ David Alexander, born on March 12, 1996. He is eight and in the 2nd grade.

~ Christopher Hans, born on June 10, 2003 at 1 lb. 14 oz. and 13 inches long.

~ Brian Jackson, born on June 10, 2003 at 1 lb. 15 oz. and 11 inches long.

~ Brooke Tyler, born on June 10, 2003 at 1 lb. 8 oz. and 11 _ inches long.

The David and Sandra Dargel Family (2004). David Alan,
Breanna, Sandra, David Alexander, Christopher, and Brian.
Photo courtesy of David and Sandra Dargel.

Brooke Tyler Dargel, at one month of age, died July 11, 2003 at the Neonatal Care Unit in Plano, Texas. We love you, Brooke, and realize we can come to you someday, but you cannot come to us. Brooke is buried at Roselawn Funeral Home & Memorial Gardens in Seagoville, Texas.

Stanley (Stan) graduated from Eagle Pass High School in 1989 and attended Midwestern State University in Wichita Falls and received a bachelor degree in radiological science in 1995. He married Teresa Thornberry on August 10, 2003. Teresa has a son, Taylor Lovell, who was born May 22, 1990 and is currently in the

9th grade in school. Stan and a business partner started a temporary staffing business in 2001. This firm focuses on placing medical professionals in local medical facilities in the North Dallas area. In addition to this small business endeavor, Stan, in partnership with his brother, Kevin, have recently kicked off another startup business venture. They started Core Publishing & Consulting Inc. on April 27, 2004, to develop and publish book projects, similar to this one, as well as market web-based continuing education courses to medical professionals.

The Stan and Teresa Peterson Family (2004). Taylor, Teresa, and Stan.

Photo courtesy of Stan and Teresa Peterson.

Our family is very close and stays in touch with each other even though we are now spread out from Florida, North Carolina, and Louisiana to Texas. We have a family reunion once a year. In 2004 Stan and Teresa hosted the reunion. We get to tell the old family stories and meet the new members that seem to continue to be added to the family tree. I recall one such story that my oldest son David told at one of those reunion gatherings. As young children, sometimes our children jumped in their beds and went to bed only after I had called downstairs several times. I would yell down the stairs and say, *"Turn over and face the wall!"* Some of them claim that to this day they can't sleep until they turn over and face the wall.

Our family has a tradition of putting on a talent show at these reunions. It is great to see all the talent distributed across the family by our gracious Lord. Of course, these times allow us to share the gospel with each other. JoAnne and I have a firm and non-negotiable goal to see each and every member of our family make it to heaven with us!

When JoAnne and I courted prior to starting our family, we had read the *Bible* together and made it a point that our future marriage was to be a three-some: JoAnne, me, and Jesus Christ in the center. We pray that each member of the family as well as the reader will adopt this practice. It will build a strong family. Amen!

JoAnne and I invested in our family in a variety of ways. When we traveled together, we listened to the gospel preachers on the radio. The children said, *"Dad could always find a gospel preacher on the radio."* I trust that God will continue to allow good gospel preaching on radio and TV.

We ate meals the old-fashioned way. There was a dinner call and everyone came to the table to eat at the same time. We shared and talked shop and school. Then we read one chapter from the

Bible and prayed. Each child had a *New Testament* that we kept in a wicker basket. The children took turns passing out the books or collecting the books. If one of the children was not paying attention to the Word or was daydreaming, it would be his or her turn to read. Sometimes they had to ask which verse we were on. This was embarrassing to them and taught them to follow along. It also greatly improved their reading skills. This approach to planting the Word in the hearts of our children was based on a man named Daniel in the *Bible. Daniel* 6:10 states:

> *"Now when Daniel knew that the writing was signed,*
> *he went into his house; and his windows being open in*
> *his chamber toward Jerusalem, he kneeled upon his*
> *knees three times a day, and prayed, and gave thanks*
> *before his God, as he did aforetime."*

Families today seem to miss these opportunities to eat together. It is a time to share the day's problems, maybe give some advice or lend a helping hand.

Years ago, there was a marketing ad that was advertising Hastings Piston Rings. This tough looking fellow was holding a set of piston rings. The caption *"Tough but oh so gentle"* was under the cartoon image of this fellow. Can we be there for our families as well, with tough love and a gentle spirit? **I learned the lesson that: "A motto for raising children is 'tough but oh so gentle.'"**

As I think of the world my family is living in today, I am in utter amazement at how our world has changed since I was born, without a doctor present and in a winter snowstorm, back in 1933! Over the years, electricity must have been the most life changing invention I have seen. I remember trimming the lamps and the lantern

TOUGH..but oh so gentle

TOUGH ON OIL-PUMPING · GENTLE ON CYLINDER WALLS

When your car first starts using too much oil, look out for worn-out piston rings. They cause oil-pumping...loss of power...destructive engine wear.

Fortunately, it's comparatively easy and inexpensive to replace worn-out piston rings—but the more you delay, the more you pay.

Keep your car out of the DANGER ZONE

Ask your next service man for a Genuine Zone check-up. And write for the free Hastings Danger Zone Book-let which shows you how to save money on engine repairs. Dept. P. Hastings Manufacturing Co., Hastings, Michigan. Hastings Ltd., Toronto.

At the first sign of oil-pumping, replace your rings with Hastings piston rings. They're engineered for replacement service. They stop oil-pumping, check cylinder wear, restore engine performance.

It's the best money you can spend on your car.

HASTINGS

STEEL-VENT PISTON RINGS

PISTON RINGS · SPARK PLUGS · OIL FILTERS · TAPPETS · GREASE

Historical Hastings Piston Ring advertisement that Hans Peterson adopted as a good motto for raising his eight children.

Illustration courtesy of Hastings Manufacturing Company and Peterson Portrait Design.

wicks and putting lamp fuel (kerosene) in them to be ready for evening. Even if you had a lantern hanging in each end of the barn, you could hardly find the cows in the middle of the barn.

One thing that electricity really changed was drilling a hole in a piece of wood. For example, repairing a hayrack that needed a bolt to hold two boards together required one to drill a hole first. In those early years on the farm, we used a hand drill with a brace and bit to manually generate the hole for the bolt on the hayrack. With electricity, we used an electric drill, and it was so fast.

Another change to the farming process was electric lights in the chicken coup. Lights on in the chicken coup all night long were a real plus because it resulted in the chickens laying more eggs.

One issue that has plagued America during my lifetime is in the area of race relations. Our family did not have problems with this race thing. We moved to south Texas to reach out to our friends south of the border as we began our new life. We loved them and their smiles and their culture. Although it is very different from my northern heritage, the Hispanics we met treated us like royalty over the years. Our children have used Spanish and the Hispanic culture in their jobs and relationships. Some married into this Hispanic tradition, further connecting our family with this culture.

I want to raise another issue of grave concern that profoundly bothers me in the world today. I am very concerned about the abortions that take place each day in the world. For years I have heard that a picture is worth a thousand words. I believe that to be true. Some pictures, however, are worth more and some are worth less. The picture shown here is worth 1,600.

Traveling through Sedalia, Missouri on U.S. 50 on a Memorial Day, a man by the name of Tom Buttram said his eyes were pulled to the side of the road to witness a panorama of Crosses that resembled Arlington National Cemetery in the front yard of **Our Savior Lutheran Church**. He got out of his car, walked over and stood among the memorial Crosses and read the sign: *"In memory of the 1,600 babies who lost their lives to abortion this morning."* Standing among the *represented babies* he read the sign again and it really did say, *"This morning!"* *"My dear God,"* he cried, *"Not this year or this month and not even this week, but —this morning!"*

He went back to get his camera, and his wife who waited in the

The front yard of Our Savior Lutheran Church in Sedalia, Missouri.
"There Is Something Tragically Wrong Here…"

Photo courtesy of Tom Buttram and Peterson Portrait Design.

car asked what the sign said. He couldn't tell her. He couldn't talk at all. He was overwhelmed. Maybe he was just too softhearted. Maybe he loved babies too much. He didn't know. But, evidently the people at Our Savior Lutheran Church felt the same thing that he did. These 1,600 images speak volumes to my heart as well.

PLEASE STOP THIS KILLING OF THE BABIES!

If anything can be done to change the hearts of mothers and fathers of this generation to stop this blood bath, I vote: *YES, stop it!*

In the world today, there are struggles with drugs, AIDS, murder, and fighting in the schools and on the streets. However, we have some good, solid, *Bible*-believing, full of faith children today, and I say "*God bless you.*" JoAnne and I trusted God and served

Him according to His Word for us as a couple and for our children and their children to come, always abounding in the work of the Lord.

JoAnne and I have relied upon two particular scripture passages to guide our family toward quality and fulfilling lives. The first is *I Corinthians* 15:58:

> *"Therefore, my beloved brethren, be ye steadfast,*
> *unmovable, always abounding in the work of the Lord,*
> *forasmuch as ye know that your labor is not in vain in*
> *the Lord."*

The second is *Proverbs* 22:6:

> *"Train up a child in the way he should go, and when he*
> *is old, he will not depart from it."*

The life lessons learned from these two verses are: *"Make sure you do the right thing as the spiritual example for your family to follow"* **and** *"Faithfully plant God's Word and His instructions in the heart of your children while they are young and they will follow God."*

CHAPTER THIRTEEN

Lessons Learned Over a Lifetime

A s I look back over my life, I am grateful for what God has provided in my life and the gift of salvation that He has given to me. The Lord has demonstrated that He is capable and willing to lead us by His spirit, in very practical ways, if we will merely yield to that voice of our *inner man* as we draw nearer to Him in our daily walk.

I have learned a number of lessons over my lifetime and hope they will enhance your quality of life in some measure. I have seventeen different life lessons learned that I have shared with you from my experiences. I learned some of these by the school of hard knocks and others through the insights given by the power of God's revelations by being born of the Spirit. Here's a quick review of these lessons learned:

1. (Chapter 1) Do not just accept your core beliefs as the foundation for your life. Research and validate these based on the Word of God—build your life on spiritual truth.

2. (Chapter 2) No matter how great your parents may be (as

mine were), you are personally responsible and accountable to build a biblically principled relationship with God
for your own life and for eternity.

3. (Chapter 4) You better believe that if you spare the rod
   you spoil the child.

4. (Chapter 4) Be honest with all men and study to show
   yourself approved unto God a workman that needeth not
   to be ashamed—rightly dividing the word of truth.

5. (Chapter 4) School is extremely important and it is worth
   the effort to study hard.

6. (Chapter 4) If at all possible, try to select a career in life
   that coincides with your personal areas of passion. This
   will increase your odds of being successful and having a
   rewarding work experience over your entire lifetime.

7. (Chapter 4) We need to watch what and how we spend
   our financial resources in life.

8. (Chapter 5) All things work together for good to them that
   love God, to them who are the called according to His
   purpose.

9. (Chapter 5) Young people can spot the genuine article and
   will bend (gravitate) toward it with the right leadership
   from key adult role models.

10. (Chapter 8) In Him (Jesus) was life and the life was the
    light of men.

11. (Chapter 8) Sometimes things turn to mud!

12. (Chapter 9) As we walk out in faith to follow God, His
    Spirit provides direction in very practical ways as He
    guides us toward His plan for our lives, as we yield to His
    path for our life.

13. (Chapter 10) God's Word and Plans withstand the trials of
    life and the test of time.

14. (Chapter 11) Be ready to meet King Jesus at any moment.
15. (Chapter 12) A motto for raising children is 'tough but oh so gentle'.
16. (Chapter 12) Make sure you do the right thing as the spiritual example for your family to follow.
17. (Chapter 12) Faithfully plant God's Word and His instructions in the heart of your children while they are young and they will follow God.

CHAPTER FOURTEEN

Concluding Remarks

As I wrap up the story of my life, I reflect on a man that God used as His instrument to cause the turning point in my life in 1965. That man (Andy) had a lasting effect on my life. He really loved God and Christ Jesus and believed the Word of God just like it is written. He challenged me. And then, he helped me to trust God and to look to Jesus for help and spiritual healing.

Dear reader, you owe it to yourself and to our God to study and read those chapters and verses that have been quoted from in this book project. *Isaiah 59:1–2* says:

> *Behold, the Lord's hand is not shortened, that it cannot save; neither his ear heavy, that it cannot hear. But your iniquities have separated between you and your God, and your sins have hid his face from you, that he will not hear."*

And, my dear friend, as Jesus said to the Jews that believed in *John 8:31–32*:

"Then said Jesus to those Jews which believed on him, If ye continue in my word, then are ye my disciples indeed. And ye shall know the truth, and the truth shall make you free."

This is God's guarantee on His plan for man. This will work for you as well!

Let me challenge you. Describe the spiritual you. Do you have peace of mind? Why or why not? I challenge anyone to try to give more than God! He will give back to you, pressed down and running over, as described in *Luke* 6:38. God's Word is true—you can take it to the bank—that is, God's storehouse.

Andy showed me the difference between *churchianity* and Christianity. This apostate church is alive and still growing, and is becoming more like the world all the time. So does religion play a role in my life? Oh, yes! Absolutely! Without Christ in my life, I would feel like this was a wasted life.

I rejoice in my observations of God at work and how His Word has changed lives. Giving out the Word, speaking with my mouth, or my handing someone a *New Testament* or a *Bible* has been the joy of *our life.* I say *our life* because Jo has always been there to say amen and has been a full partner throughout our fifty years of marriage. She would say, *"Yes, we can do more. We can handle that. And, God has always come through."*

Ephesians 3:16 says: *"That he would grant you, according to the riches of his glory, to be strengthened with might by his Spirit in the inner man."*

That *inner man* spoken of here is the real you. You and I are either hooked on this world or hooked on the 'Kingdom of God' by the Holy Ghost.

I got bent one day on my knees in prayer to God. I called to Him and said, *"I don't know where I am. Lord help me—Lord, save me—Lord, come into my heart and be my God and my Savior. Help me to live my life for you."*

It really works, folks. Try Him! Nothing is impossible with my God. *The Lord bent my soul—let God bend yours toward the truth of His Word and His Spirit.*

NOTES

ILLUSTRATIONS
1. Most of the photographs courtesy of Peterson Portrait Design and others were provided as a courtesy of other members of my family.
2. Hastings Piston Rings Illustration courtesy of Hastings Manufacturing Company.
3. Our Savior Lutheran Church, Cross Illustration Photograph courtesy of Tom Buttram.
4. ClipArt from MasterClips™, 101,000 Premium Image Collection, Volume I, International Microcomputer Software Inc., 1996.
5. Final manuscript photographs and illustrations prepared for typesetting courtesy of Rod Brink Photography.

FOREWORD
1. *The King James Study Bible*, Thomas Nelson Publishers, *Psalm* 37:23.

ACKNOWLEDGMENTS
2. *The King James Study Bible*, Thomas Nelson Publishers, *John* 1:4.

DEDICATION
1. *The King James Study Bible*, Thomas Nelson Publishers, *Psalm* 102:18.

PREFACE
1. *The King James Study Bible*, Thomas Nelson Publishers, *Romans* 3:23.
2. *The King James Study Bible*, Thomas Nelson Publishers, *John* 3:16.
3. *The King James Study Bible*, Thomas Nelson Publishers, *I John* 1:7–9.

4. *The King James Study Bible*, Thomas Nelson Publishers, *Zechariah* 9:13.

CHAPTER 2

1. *Hang On The Potatoes*, Erling H. Peterson, 1982, Eakin Publications, Inc., pp. 36–37, 43–46, 68–72.
2. Memorial: Lavilla C. Peterson, Hoplin Funeral Home, Glenwood, Minnesota.
3. *A New Guide and Almanac: Religions Of America*, Leo Rosten (ed.), Simon & Schuster, Inc., pp. 156–162.
4. *Handbook of Denominations in the United States*, new eighth edition, Frank S. Mead, Samuel S. Hill (rev. ed.), Abingdon Press, pp. 142–144.
5. *New 20th-Century Encyclopedia of Religious Knowledge*, second edition, J. D. Douglas (ed.), Baker Book House, p. 526.
6. *Luther's Small Catechism with Explanations*, Concordia Publishing House, pp. 9–12, 16, 21–24, 28–29, 99, 105, 115–116, 144, 199–212, 236–237, 241–242.
7. *The King James Study Bible*, Thomas Nelson Publishers, *Matthew* 28:19.
8. *The King James Study Bible*, Thomas Nelson Publishers, *Luke* 22:7–20.
9. *The King James Study Bible*, Thomas Nelson Publishers, *Matthew* 26:17–29.
10. *The King James Study Bible*, Thomas Nelson Publishers, *Mark* 14:12–25.
11. *The King James Study Bible*, Thomas Nelson Publishers, *John* 8:31–32.
12. *The King James Study Bible*, Thomas Nelson Publishers, *Philippians* 2:12.

CHAPTER 4

1. *The King James Study Bible*, Thomas Nelson Publishers, *Proverbs* 13:24.
2. *The King James Study Bible*, Thomas Nelson Publishers, *II Timothy* 2:15.
3. *The World Almanac and Book of Facts 2003*, World Almanac Books, pp. 533–534.

CHAPTER 5

1. *The King James Study Bible*, Thomas Nelson Publishers, *Romans* 8:28.
2. *Great People of the 20th Century*, Times Books, pp. 142–143.
3. *My Soul More Bent*, Allen Lee of the ELC.
4. *The King James Study Bible*, Thomas Nelson Publishers, *Zechariah* 9:13.

CHAPTER 6

1. *The King James Study Bible*, Thomas Nelson Publishers, *Acts* 4:12.

CHAPTER 8

1. *The King James Study Bible*, Thomas Nelson Publishers, *Galatians* 3:24.
2. *The King James Study Bible*, Thomas Nelson Publishers, *John* 1:4.
3. *The King James Study Bible*, Thomas Nelson Publishers, *John* 1:12.
4. *The King James Study Bible*, Thomas Nelson Publishers, *Revelation* 22:17.
5. *The King James Study Bible*, Thomas Nelson Publishers, *John* 3:4.
6. *The King James Study Bible*, Thomas Nelson Publishers, *Romans* 6:11–14, 23.
7. *The King James Study Bible*, Thomas Nelson Publishers, *I John* 5:13.
8. *The King James Study Bible*, Thomas Nelson Publishers, *Romans* 3:22–26.
9. *The King James Study Bible*, Thomas Nelson Publishers, *Ephesians* 3:16.
10. *The King James Study Bible*, Thomas Nelson Publishers, *Exodus* 20:7.
11. *The King James Study Bible*, Thomas Nelson Publishers, *Hebrews* 11:1–40.
12. *The King James Study Bible*, Thomas Nelson Publishers, *Matthew* 16:26.
13. *The King James Study Bible*, Thomas Nelson Publishers, *Genesis* 28:10–18.
14. *The King James Study Bible*, Thomas Nelson Publishers, *Job* 42:10–11.

CHAPTER 9

1. *The King James Study Bible*, Thomas Nelson Publishers, *Galatians* 5:22–23.

2. *The King James Study Bible*, Thomas Nelson Publishers, *Titus* 3:5.

3. *The Full Life Study Bible, King James Version*, Donald C. Stamps, Zondervan Publishing House, p. 1597.

4. *The Mackintosh Treasury, Miscellaneous Writings*, C. H. Mackintosh, Loizeaux Brothers, p. 617.

5. *The King James Study Bible*, Thomas Nelson Publishers, *Romans* 3:9–18.

6. *Romans: Inside Commentaries*, H. A. Ironside, revised edition, Loizeaux, Nepture, p. 25.

7. *Statement of Faith and Discipline for Original Free Will Baptists of North Carolina*, 3rd Edition, 1961, Chapter XIII ("Perseverance of the Saints"), p. 30.

8. *The King James Study Bible*, Thomas Nelson Publishers, *Philippians* 2:12.

9. *The King James Study Bible*, Thomas Nelson Publishers, *Hebrews* 12:22–24, 28.

10. *The King James Study Bible*, Thomas Nelson Publishers, *Revelation* 1:6.

11. *The King James Study Bible*, Thomas Nelson Publishers, *Mark* 16:15–20.

12. *The King James Study Bible*, Thomas Nelson Publishers, *I Thessalonians* 5:23.

13. *The King James Study Bible*, Thomas Nelson Publishers, *John* 16:13.

14. *Profiles of Lutherans in the USA*, Carl F. Reuss, Augsburg Publishing House, pp. 19–20.

15. *The King James Study Bible*, Thomas Nelson Publishers, *Acts* 8:36–38.

16. *The King James Study Bible*, Thomas Nelson Publishers, *I Corinthians* 8:9–13.

17. *The King James Study Bible*, Thomas Nelson Publishers, *Acts* 8:37.

18. *The King James Study Bible*, Thomas Nelson Publishers, *Romans* 6:1–2, 4–5, 11.

19. *The King James Study Bible*, Thomas Nelson Publishers, *II Corinthians* 5:21.

20. *The King James Study Bible*, Thomas Nelson Publishers, *Matthew* 3:13–17.

21. *The King James Study Bible*, Thomas Nelson Publishers, *Matthew* 28:18–20.

22. *The King James Study Bible*, Thomas Nelson Publishers, *Mark* 16:16.
23. *The Full Life Study Bible*, Donald C. Stamps, Zondervan Publishing House, p. 1787.
24. *The King James Study Bible*, Thomas Nelson Publishers, *Matthew* 26:26–29.
25. *The King James Study Bible*, Thomas Nelson Publishers, *Mark* 14:22–25.
26. *The King James Study Bible*, Thomas Nelson Publishers, *Luke* 22:15–20.
27. *The King James Study Bible*, Thomas Nelson Publishers, *I Corinthians* 11:23–25.
28. *The King James Study Bible*, Thomas Nelson Publishers, *Acts* 8:29.
29. *The King James Study Bible*, Thomas Nelson Publishers, *Acts* 16:9–10.
30. *The King James Study Bible*, Thomas Nelson Publishers, *I John* 3:20–21.
31. *The King James Study Bible*, Thomas Nelson Publishers, *Galatians* 5:16–25.

CHAPTER 10
1. *The World Almanac and Book of Facts 2003*, World Almanac Books, p. 536.
2. *The King James Study Bible*, Thomas Nelson Publishers, *Acts* 1:8.
3. *The King James Study Bible*, Thomas Nelson Publishers, *John* 1:12.
4. *The King James Study Bible*, Thomas Nelson Publishers, *John* 3:16.
5. *The King James Study Bible*, Thomas Nelson Publishers, *John* 5:24.
6. *The King James Study Bible*, Thomas Nelson Publishers, *Acts* 3:19.
7. *The King James Study Bible*, Thomas Nelson Publishers, *Romans* 3:19–24.
8. *The King James Study Bible*, Thomas Nelson Publishers, *Romans* 12:1.
9. *The King James Study Bible*, Thomas Nelson Publishers, *Galatians* 3:24.

10. *The King James Study Bible*, Thomas Nelson Publishers, *Ephesians* 3:16.
11. *The King James Study Bible*, Thomas Nelson Publishers, *II Timothy* 2:4.
12. *The King James Study Bible*, Thomas Nelson Publishers, *I John* 1:7, 9.
13. *The King James Study Bible*, Thomas Nelson Publishers, *I John* 5:13.
14. *The King James Study Bible*, Thomas Nelson Publishers, *Revelation* 3:20.
15. *The King James Study Bible*, Thomas Nelson Publishers, *Luke* 23:1–56.
16. *The King James Study Bible*, Thomas Nelson Publishers, *Luke* 24:1–53.
17. *The King James Study Bible*, Thomas Nelson Publishers, *Isaiah* 55:7.
18. *The King James Study Bible*, Thomas Nelson Publishers, *John* 8:31–32, 36.
19. *The King James Study Bible*, Thomas Nelson Publishers, *Hebrews* 13:2, 5.
20. *The King James Study Bible*, Thomas Nelson Publishers, *Luke* 23:39–43.
21. *The King James Study Bible*, Thomas Nelson Publishers, *John* 8:36.
22. "Estimated number of *New Testaments* distributed as part of jail ministry," Kevin Peterson, May 25, 2004.
23. *Modern Vet Practice*, "Rabies Protection: A Better Approach", 1980, pp. 455–457.
24. *Melodies of Praise*, "A Crown of Thorns," Ira Stanphill Gospel Publishing House, 1952.
25. *The King James Study Bible*, Thomas Nelson Publishers, *I Corinthians* 11:23–26.
26. *The King James Study Bible*, Thomas Nelson Publishers, *Luke* 23:34.
27. *The King James Study Bible*, Thomas Nelson Publishers, *Luke* 22:18.

CHAPTER 11
1. Memorial: Curtis Dale Peterson, Alexander City, Alabama.

CHAPTER 12

1. Advertisement for *Hastings Piston Rings*, (permission granted on 11-25-2003 by Hastings to Dr. Hans Peterson for the sole use on this illustration within this book project).
2. Permission granted by Tom Buttram to use his photograph of the "Cross illustration" outside of Our Savior Lutheran Church in Sedalia, Missouri.
3. *The King James Study Bible*, Thomas Nelson Publishers, *I Corinthians* 15:58.
4. *The King James Study Bible*, Thomas Nelson Publishers, *Proverbs* 22:6.

CHAPTER 13

1. *The King James Study Bible*, Thomas Nelson Publishers, *Proverbs* 13:24.
2. *The King James Study Bible*, Thomas Nelson Publishers, *II Timothy* 2:15.
3. *The King James Study Bible*, Thomas Nelson Publishers, *Romans* 8:28.
4. Advertisement for *Hastings Piston Rings* (permission granted on 11-25-2003 by Hastings to Dr. Hans Peterson for the sole use on this illustration within this book project).

CHAPTER 14

1. *The King James Study Bible*, Thomas Nelson Publishers, *Isaiah* 59:1–2.
2. *The King James Study Bible*, Thomas Nelson Publishers, *John* 8:31–32.
3. *The King James Study Bible*, Thomas Nelson Publishers, *Luke* 6:38.
4. *The King James Study Bible*, Thomas Nelson Publishers, *Ephesians* 3:16.

AUTHOR

The author of this book, Hans Peterson, DVM, brings his background as a husband of fifty years, a father of eight children, Doctor of Veterinary Medicine, small business owner/operator, and jail minister to this project. He married his high school sweetheart, JoAnne Peterson. In addition to their eight children, he and his wife have twenty-one grandchildren and five great-grandchildren. All of their children attended some level of college and these children have accumulated seven undergraduate and four graduate level degrees amongst themselves.

The author was born in Minnesota, but spent a large portion of his life on the Texas–Mexico border. Dr. Peterson has practiced veterinary medicine for the past forty-four years, in four separate practices: two in Minnesota and two in Texas. In addition to these veterinary practices, he built two feed store operations that were sold to new owners as well as ran a family hog farm operation while in Texas. And finally, he served for nearly twenty-two years as a lay minister in the local jail in Eagle Pass, Texas and in a penitentiary in Piedras Negras, Coahuila, Mexico. As part of this ministry, he distributed an estimated 30 thousand *New Testament* and 3 thousand complete *Bibles* to Mexico and South America by the inmates he came in contact with through these services every Sunday. While no longer serving on the mission field, the author (at age seventy-one) is still operating a veterinary clinic in North Texas and enjoying his large, and ever increasing, family.

Give the Gift of "Inspiration" to your Friends and Family

You can find this book at your local Bookstore or Order Here

To order your copies, Log-on to www.core-publishing.com

You may also place an order by calling 1-214-926-4742
or faxing this order form to 1-972-243-5854

Allow 3 weeks for delivery.

RETAIL PRICE PLUS SHIPPING & HANDLING	QUANTITY	SUB-TOTAL
Retail Price $19.95 (US Dollars) *My Soul Got Bent* ISBN 1-933079-01-0		
Include $4.00 Shipping & Handling for one book, and $2.00 for each additional book		
Sub-Total	N/A	
Applicable Sales Tax (Texas Residents @ 8.25%)	N/A	
TOTAL		

Texas residents must include applicable state sales tax.

Canadian orders must include payment in US funds.

For purchases of five books or more, please call for any standard pricing discounts.

My check or money order for $_____ is enclosed.

[Payments must accompany orders, no CODs]

Please charge my   ☐ **Visa**   ☐ **MasterCard**   ☐ **American Express**

NAME:_____

ORGANIZATION: _____

ADDRESS: _____

CITY / STATE / ZIP: _____

PHONE:_____   E-MAIL:_____

CARD #_____

EXP. DATE: _____   SIGNATURE: _____

MAKE YOUR CHECK PAYABLE AND RETURN TO:

Core Publishing & Consulting, Inc

Core Publishing & Consulting, Inc.
Stan J. Peterson, President
13016 Bee Street, Suite 208
Dallas, TX 75234-6158